Copyright 2008, 2009 Will Carpenter
All rights reserved.
HistoryWorks Publishing
P.O. Box 3312, Cookeville, Tennessee 38502
http://historyworksbooks.com
Printed in the United States of America
Second Edition, March 2009

10 9 8 7 6 5 4 3 2

The advice and information in this book are believed to be true and accurate at the date of printing, but neither the author nor publisher can accept any legal responsibility or liability for any errors or omissions.

No part of this publication my be reproduced, stored in a retrieval system or transmitted in any form or by any means, electronic or mechanical, photocopying, recording or otherwise without the express written permission of the author.

Library of Congress Cataloging-in-Publication Data

  Carpenter
  "The Life & Times Of...." : Researching and Writing American Local History / by Will Carpenter
    p. cm.
  Second ed.
  Includes bibliographical references and index.
  Contents: Researching and writing American local history –The influence of English and European history on American local history, the American community and its influence, the historical method, using computers for historical research, interpreting and writing local and family history.
  ISBN 10: 0-61527271-1
  ISBN 13: 978-061527271-9 (pbk.)
  1. History. 2. Genealogy and Local History. 3. Historiography. 4. Local History. I. Carpenter, Will, 1952-. II. Title.
F1-975.C37
973.07—dc21

                                                                 2009920634

"THE LIFE & TIMES OF...."

"THE LIFE & TIMES OF..."

RESEARCHING AND WRITING AMERICAN LOCAL HISTORY

Second Edition

Will Carpenter

HistoryWorks

Sweet Patricia

&

The Cats

Table of Contents

ACKNOWLEDGEMENTS — XIII

PREFACE — XV

CHAPTER 1   THE SEARCH FOR LOCAL HISTORY BEGINS WITH WHAT WE KNOW ... AND THEN SOME — 17

   Introduction to Local History — *17*

   History Is Not A Vacuum — *20*

   (Almost) All of Us Came From Somewhere Else — *47*

   The Past Was Different and Differences Define the Past — *50*

   Recognition of the Historical Process — *53*

CHAPTER 2 ELEMENTS OF LOCAL HISTORY: PEOPLE, PLACE ... AND COMMUNITY?   61

    The Element of Place   67

    The People   75

    Community as a Separate Entity   77

CHAPTER 3 BEGINNING TO DO HISTORY: SOURCES, QUESTIONS AND THE HISTORICAL METHOD   91

    Beginning to Do History: Historical Sources   92

    Credibility of the Historical Source: Critical Thinking   95

    Supposition, Research & Hypothesis   116

CHAPTER 4 THE COMPUTER IN HISTORICAL RESEARCH   129

    Doing History By The Numbers: Quantitative Analysis   130

    GIS Systems   153

CHAPTER 5 SYNTHESIS: TURNING RESEARCH INTO HISTORY   157

    The Historical Imagination   159

Meaning & Theories of Meaning: Interpreting Sources	163
Writing the History	168
Fifty Years	173
FURTHER READING	179
APPENDIX 1: ONLINE RESOURCES IN THE UNITED STATES	185
APPENDIX 2: ONLINE RESOURCES OUTSIDE THE UNITED STATES	207
INDEX	

Table of Illustrations & Figures

Map of the Louisiana Purchase (Image Courtesy of the National Park Service)   55

Women voters (Courtesy of the Library of Congress)... 76

Gregory Gold Diggings,Colorado May 1859 (Image Courtesy of the Library of Congress)   78

Manzanar War Relocation Center, 1943 (Photo by Ansel Adams, Courtesy of the Library of Congress)   83

Figure 1.1 Major European Wars, 1492-1815..............47

Figure 1.2 European Famines 1590-1900.................38

Figure 1.3 European Pandemics, 1349-1831   43

Figure 3.1 If a Theory Has Less Speculative

Baggage..120

Figure 3.2 Validation of a Hypothesis....... 125

Figure 5.1 Interval Data. Data sets illustrative only 132

Figure 5.2 Ratio of Bars to Bar/Restaurants at Intersections of Bourbon Street and the Level of Patron Sobriety at those locations. Source: Street Information, AAA Map of New Orleans.   133

Figure 5.3 Data Types.   134

Figure 5.4 - Tabular Format, Time-Series, Hourly Wages – Laborer..136

Figure 5.5 Time-Series graph, Hourly Wages 137

Figure 5.6 Time-Series, Cost of Bread.   138

Figure 5.7 Hours Worked For 1 lb. of Bread. .   139

Figure 5.8 Illustration of Case. .   140

Figure 5.9 Illustration of Variable.   140

Figure 5.10 The data matrix and Components......141

Figure 5.11 Data Matrix of Imaginary Names   145

Figure 5.12. Distribution of Given Names

.... 145

Figure 5.13 Frequency of Given Names   146

Figure 5.14. Frequency distribution Given Names   146

Figure 5.15 Determining the Mean Value (in thousands of dollars) of housing in   148

Figure 5.16 The median in this example is 149

Figure 5.17 Frequency Distribution of Housing Values in fictional Neighborhood........................ 150

Figure 5.18 Frequency Distribution of Housing Values in a fictional Neighborhood..............................150

Acknowledgements

Patricia, whose skilled eyes found errors, even after proofreading, that would have otherwise never been noticed;; Judy Duke, who made sure that history wouldn't suffer; Dr. Robert P. Swierenga, a giant standing on the shoulders of giants, for his gracious encouragement and assistance; Dr George Richardson, another giant, whose kindness was invaluable; Dr. Steven Kreis, who taught me the consequences of medieval warfare; Linda Barnickel, of the Nashville, Tennessee, Public Library, who reminded me that historians, librarians and archivists ride the peak seat of Eternity's engine; Matthew Pearce of Her Majesty's Office of Public Sector Information, who steered me in the right direction at a critical juncture during the first few tries; Sam Jones, whose unlikely name is no alias and who taught me the meaning of JDLR...and Captain Bartholomew Gosnold, who started it all.

Preface

Since the Romans perfected bureaucracy, governments large and small have kept copious records of the minutiae of the daily life of their citizens attesting the facts of a place, whether a street, a neighborhood, a village, or some other manageable bit of real estate, and the people who occupy that place. Those two elements, people and place, are the essential components of local history. The people may have shared an occupation or skills within an occupation or profession, or they might have physical characteristics in common or a cultural or historical heritage that ultimately became American. Without those connections, the one thing they all have in common is that they lived in the same specific place. To find out how that came to be true requires research.

In the United States, many of the oldest buildings were constructed when America was a group of English colonies. Some aspects of local history have been ignored or misunderstood, perhaps because the answers to these questions lay more than 3,000 miles and several hundred years away.

Today, people are beginning to realize that history begins

in their own back yards. They are asking crucial questions about the buildings, their construction, their builders and their occupants; who these people were, what they did, how they thought and believed, why they lived here and how did they live.

This book begins with *us*: how we got here, what we did and why we did it then gives you the tools to discover and make your own contribution to that history.

Chapter 1

The Search for Local History Begins With What We Know ... and Then Some

History is the sum total of the things that could have been avoided.
~Konrad Adenauer

American history is based on a true story. While we might have studied American history in school, and while we might remember some of it, finding answers in local history or family history means that we have to recognize that history is not a vacuum, that almost all of us are from someplace else and finally, that the past is different.

Introduction to Local History

Local history is about people and the place they occupy, both as individuals and ultimately, as a group: a community growing out of the similarities, disparities and relationships that form over the years within the group and beyond. These three elements, people place and community, provide the evidentiary tapestry from which the local historian may draw; however, because of the richness and diversity of that evidence, the practice of local history may frequently seem like trying to drink from a fire hose.

Researching and writing local history requires only two things: curiosity about a place and the people in it, and a desire to find out all available information about that place and those people. Where did they live and why? How and when they lived, how they worked and played, their associations and groupings at the local level, how and where they worshipped, what their view of the world was, what they thought – in short what, they and their locale were like, and how they and their corner of the world was different from today.

The first thing local historians should learn is that most of their work has been done at least once before. Many counties, cities and towns in America have had at least one local history written for each generation they have been settled. Depending on the part of the United States, older histories can offer the local or family historian the opportunity to read documents formerly in an unfamiliar language or script without having to take classes in Medieval Latin or palaeography.

In the past, the task of writing a local history was usually entrusted to a learned person who lived locally, who had some idea of how to do research and perhaps even had first hand knowledge of some of the people or events described. This makes previous editions of the local history invaluable for the local historian, simply because (so it would seem) most of the work is already done. Or has it? To begin writing a history – family or local, the skills are the same – you have to know where to start. If you're doing a family history, your starting place is the person about whom you are writing. If you're doing local history, the starting point is the place. The next steps are the real work of writing a history.

Historical research is simple and straightforward on the surface, requiring seven steps and note cards. Lots of note cards:

Assemble the research materials available

Delve into the existing research, finding information pertaining to the subject

Decide which historical sources – documents, films, photographs, old letters or diaries, oral history, eyewitness testimony or archaeological evidence – are pertinent to your study

Decide which of the available historical sources are both credible and reliable

Formulate an idea – a hypothesis – of what each piece means in the overall scheme of your study

19

Test these hypotheses for validity using the historical method

Determine the meaning of the information presented by the valid hypotheses

The final goal is, of course, to write the history, one based on the validated hypotheses and their meanings.

Is this much effort worth it?

Yes.

History Is Not A Vacuum

It wasn't until 1968 that America had existed longer as an independent country than as a colony of another country. The history of the United States is so closely linked with the history of nearly every European country that the historian E. B. Greene described America as the "record of European enterprise on American soil."[1] Even earlier, Thomas Paine said in his pre-Revolutionary War pamphlet *Common Sense*, "America is the child not of England, but of Europe."

European events continued to physically shape America long after its independence from England and sometimes, decisions made by the various European powers years before American independence continued to have an effect on America well into the next century. Two examples of this are found in the existence of the states of Maine and Vermont.

The thirteen original colonies were New Hampshire, Massachusetts, Rhode Island, Connecticut, New York, Pennsylvania, Maryland, Delaware, Virginia, North Carolina, South Carolina, New Jersey and Georgia. Until 1777, Vermont was part of New York. In 1764, King George III settled a boundary dispute between New York and New Hampshire in such a way that the area now known as Vermont was no longer a part of New Hampshire, but part of Albany County, New York. This boundary later became the boundary between New Hampshire and Vermont. New York refused to honor land titles issued by New Hampshire and dissatisfied citizens of the area organized opposition, which led to the creation of Vermont in 1777.[2]

Maine was part of Massachusetts until 1820, when it became a separate state as part of the Missouri Compromise. In 1819, Alabama, a slave state, was admitted to the Union, making the number of slave states and free states equal. Missouri had petitioned for statehood, to be admitted as a slave state, which would have shifted the balance of slave and free states in the Senate to favour the slave states. To allow Missouri to enter the Union, an additional free state would have to be created; the resulting compromise separated Maine from Massachusetts and admitted it to the Union as a free state in 1820, and Missouri was admitted to the Union in 1821. After the admissions of Maine and Missouri to the Union, no other states were admitted until Arkansas was admitted as a slave state in 1836 and Michigan in 1837 as a free state. Other events occurring in Europe had curious results for the United States.

The 1783 Peace of Paris that ended the American Revolution and the 1763 Treaty of Paris together held interesting consequences for the United States in 1803.[3]

In 1763 the Treaty of Paris ended the Seven Years War. England signed the Treaty, ending hostilities with France, Austria, and Russia. England gained control of French Canada and Florida. France gave Spain LaSalle's claim of 1682, creating a Spanish colony between the 50th parallel in North America and Tierra del Fuego at the southernmost point of South America.

The 1783 Peace of Paris officially recognized "13 United States" rather than "13 United Colonies," formally ending the American War of Independence. This same treaty ceded the Northwest Territory (the future states of Ohio, Indiana, Wisconsin, Michigan and Illinois) to the United States and returned all the territory east of the Mississippi River and south of the 31st parallel ("the Floridas") to Spain.

The colonial economy in New Spain (Spanish Louisiana and the lands to the north) was in shambles and on 11 January 1784, the Spanish government dispatched a ship, El Cazador, laden with 450,000 pesos of silver reales from Vera Cruz to New Orleans. The ship sank in a tremendous storm and in 1800 Spain transferred 'the Floridas' and LaSalle's Louisiana back to France by the "secret" Treaty of San Ildelfonso.

In 1802, President Thomas Jefferson learned about this secret treaty and in letter to Robert Livingston, the U.S. minister to France, in April 1802, Jefferson wrote:

> "There is on the globe one single spot, the possessor of which is our natural and habitual enemy. It is New Orleans, through which the produce of three-eighths of our territory must pass to market, and from its fertility it will ere long yield more than half of our whole produce, and contain more than half of our inhabitants. France, placing herself in that door, assumes to us the attitude of defiance."

The only recourse, Jefferson continued, would be to "marry ourselves to the British fleet and nation." Jefferson, ever the politician, also pointed out that,

> "If France considers Louisiana, however, as indispensable for her views, she might perhaps be willing to look about for arrangements which might reconcile it to our interests. If anything could do this, it would be the ceding to us the island of New Orleans and the Floridas."[4]

Livingston had been a member of the Committee of Five that drafted the Declaration of Independence and, as Chancellor of New York, had administered the oath of office to George Washington. It is unknown whether Napoleon or his foreign minister, Charles Maurice de Tallyrand, actually saw this letter, but Livingston was no stranger to political intrigue.

"The Life & Times Of..."

As a consequence, wars in Europe, two treaties written twenty years apart, a collapsing Spanish colonial economy, a winter storm in the Gulf of Mexico, a third treaty – supposedly secret – and the lingering animosities of the American Revolution and a liberal helping of astute political maneuvering combined to result in the Louisiana Purchase, effectively doubling the size of the United States.

What effect did these two seemingly disparate events have on people? We know that the French Protestants, the

Awaiting Examination, Ellis Island," (Courtesy of the Library of Congress)

Huguenots, settled in New Amsterdam, the Dutch colony that later became the City of New York. They also founded

New Rochelle, New York, and New Paltz, New York, where the oldest street in the United States is still lined with the original stone houses. They settled in Pennsylvania, Virginia and Charleston, South Carolina, where the oldest continuously functioning Huguenot congregation in the United States is still active today.

This is important to the researcher because the French did not permit Huguenots to settle in New France. They were unable to do so until after a large part of it was acquired by the United States – as the Louisiana Purchase. Such a fact might confirm or deny a questioned element of family or local history, even though it seems far outside the bounds of either. It fact also points out two important concepts, one being the idea that people can be unwitting witnesses to history in spite of themselves and the principle that, while the local historian must attend to local history, the local historian must be mindful of the larger historical picture.

As an exercise, the reader might attempt to divine the connection between the abolition of slavery in the United Kingdom, and the War of 1812.

A Brief History Of England...

English history is an important – but often ignored – element in the study of American local history. The Founding Fathers were all born English citizens. Their attitudes and worldview, a great portion of which stemmed from and are reflected in the early history of America.

"The Life & Times Of..."

Much of our culture and many of our traditions stem directly from this early relationship to England and English culture. While the following history is very brief, it should prove sufficient for the purposes of American local history.

Between about 300 and 1087, many of the fundamental characteristics of society took shape. By 550, the first communities that would think of themselves as 'English' had been established and trade with other cultures in Europe and the Mediterranean began. The monastic culture began to grow in England and Ireland. By 750, northeastern England had become a center of intellectual

activity. Kingship and government grew in scope, and the feudalistic warrior society, with its elements of patronage –

the gifts bestowed by the king were called benefices – and obligation, alliances-by-marriage and blood feuds began to develop. The concept of rewards for service and obligations of service became more formalized under the feudal system with specific rewards balanced by specific obligations.

As early as 850, Viking invasions had begun, causing the creation of a unified England under Alfred the Great (reigned 871-899) and his heirs. English kings forged an increasingly coherent government on a national and regional level and local inhabitants came under the control of lesser nobility who organized self-contained farming communities.

Between 900 and 1330, more happened than the Norman Conquest of 1066. Market towns were founded and a commercial mentality began to appear. Local churches emerged, and attempts to create a literate society began which in turn created new institutions and administered them in more regular and bureaucratic ways. More land was settled as the population expanded, but because of the feudal nature of ownership – the king owns it all, and gives feuds, or fiefs to lesser nobles – the lords strengthened their cultural dominance over the peasants.

The period between 1330 and 1550 was marked by the first continent-wide famines. Early 14th Century Welsh revolts saw the killing of two Welsh kings but the Welsh resisted English aggression. The Black Death of 1348-1349 killed one-third or more of the population. The

"The Life & Times Of..."

Peasants' Revolt of 1381 was a response to an additional poll tax to finance the Hundred Years War (see Figure 2.1). The Hundred Years War (1337-1453) gave England spectacular victories in France – like Agincourt – that still reverberate today in law and theatre: the Agincourt Indentures are the first recorded indentures for military service and the "band of brothers" speech in Shakespeare's *Henry V* is well known. During this same period, Richard II (1367-1400) was deposed as king and his successors descended into factionalism in the Wars of the Roses, when monarchical power revived under the Yorkists and then the Tudors.

In 1534, Henry VIII broke with the Catholic Church and established the Church of England.

In spite of these royal shenanigans, industry grew, living standards rose and economic opportunities for women widened while the English crown created one of the most effective governments in Europe by acquiring the cooperation of the local elite in developing a Parliament. The beginnings of the Renaissance appeared. The next two centuries of English history were the play set upon the stage created by the foregoing twelve:

- Elizabeth Tudor, daughter of Henry VIII, became Queen Elizabeth I in a time of war, intrigue, pirates and expansion toward Empire;
- Charles I, stepping onto a scaffold in Whitehall in 1649 having been overthrown by

Cromwell and Parliament in the English Civil Wars; the Commonwealth which resulted failed in 1660, and the monarchy was restored under Charles II, who reigned until 1685, when he was succeeded by King James II.
- The Navigation Act of 1651 was intended to protect English shipping from rising Dutch trade. It prevented shippers in America from using any but English ships to transport goods to England ports and was the first of a series of portage laws.
- The First Navigation Act of 1660 added cotton, sugar, tobacco, cotton and indigo to the list of prohibited cargoes and was expanded in the Navigation Acts of 1662, 1663, 1670 and 1673, each of which was successively restrictive on colonial trade through shipping.
- 1696 The Act to Prevent Frauds and Abuses required all foreign goods coming to America be shipped through English Ports, regardless of point of origin.
- 1733 The Molasses Act raised the duties on French West Indian Sugar and forced American colonists to buy the more expensive sure from the British West Indies, resulting in extensive smuggling and vigorous efforts made to prevent smuggling in the colonies after 1765 led to arbitrary seizures of American ships.

"The Life & Times Of..."

In 1688, The 'Glorious Revolution' entrenched parliament at the center of British government and overthrew King James II, grandson of Mary, Queen of Scots and brother of Charles II. Prince William of Orange (whose father, Frederick Henry of Orange successfully separated the Netherlands from Spain under the Peace of Westphalia) and his wife, Mary (Mary II, Protestant daughter of James II and the blood sovereign) replaced James II on the British throne. Mary died in 1694 and following the death of King William in 1702, Mary's sister Queen Anne assumed the throne and was succeeded by her son, who became the first of the kings named George, one of whom – George III – reigned England and the colonies – with ever increasing strictures – during the American Revolution

...And Why They Immigrated.

There was no "society," the work would be backbreaking, the natives were probably hostile, and less than fifty percent of those coming to the New World would survive the first year. Even so, they came, leaving the historian to ask, "Why?"

Oppression, Greed & Opportunity

Oppression, greed and opportunity have played a major role in the immigration history of the United States almost since its beginning. Many Americans associate the story of the Pilgrims, who founded Plymouth Colony in Massachusetts in 1620, with refugees coming to America seeking religious freedom.

In fact, the Pilgrims were English Separatists who followed the teachings of Richard Clyfton, parson at All Saints Parish Church in Babworth, East Retford; and Nottinghamshire, England. Unlike the Puritans, who generally stayed in England and maintained their membership and allegiance to the Church of England (although there were 35 Puritans aboard the *Mayflower* with the Pilgrims) the Separatists first fled to the Netherlands avoid religious persecution. According to William Bradford, later Governor of Plymouth Colony,

> "...After these things [referring to the fining and imprisonment of prominent Separatists] they could not long continue in any peaceable condition, but were hunted & persecuted on every side, so as their former afflictions were but as flea-bitings in comparison of these which now came upon them. For some were taken & clapt up in prison, others had their houses besett & watcht night and day, & hardly escaped their hands; and ye most were faine to flie & leave their howses & habitations, and the means of their livelehood."[15]

The members of the group were unable to procure the necessary papers to leave England and in 1608, after several abortive attempts, about 150 of the congregation arrived in Amsterdam where they joined others. By 1619, a lack of funds, a flagging truce in the Eighty Years War and the Dutch revolt against the Spanish drove the members to solicit a patent for lands in the American colonies[10] so that they might enter into negotiations with the London & Virginia Company, which administered Virginia colonies. The land grant wasn't issued until the Plymouth Council for New England received its charter in late 1620 – while the Mayflower was in transit – and was for territory north of the Virginia colony, to be called New England.

By this time, the London & Virginia Company had additional investors in the venture who insisted on some rather onerous changes to the contract with the *Mayflower*'s passengers: at the end of the seven year term of the contract, one-half the settled land and property would revert to the investors and, further, that the settlers would have only one day per week to attend personal business.

When the Pilgrims went to Amsterdam, they were seeking religious freedom. When they sailed for America, they were seeking freedom from the Eighty Years War and poverty and had become indentured to the London Company. After anchoring in Provincetown Harbor, several passengers who were aware of the terms of the London Company contract and aware that the patent was not yet  in place suggested that, without the patent they were free to do as they pleased and to ignore the contract with the London Company. The Mayflower Compact, a cooperative agreement between the settlers, was drafted and ratified by a majority vote of the adult male passengers.[16]

Slavery & Indentured Servitude

Between 1607 and 1760, fewer than one million people came to America. About six hundred thousand were European, nearly all British, and of those who were British, nearly all were English. The balance – between three and four hundred thousand – were Africans. Of the Europeans about half, including the British, were in enforced servitude of one form or another and all of the Africans were slaves. Free colonists made up only about 28% of the population.[17] Many Europeans – nearly one half of all white immigrants – came to America as indentured servants; most were Scottish, English, and German.

The status of an indentured servant provided these immigrants with an opportunity, upon completion of their service, to return to their lives as free citizens, unlike those held in slavery. Freed indentured servants from Virginia and South Carolina originally settled the state of North Carolina. Some made significant contributions to the arts, sciences and industry, like Nathaniel Bowditch, the author of *The American Practical Navigator*, a major volume on the mathematics of ship navigation, still in use today.

(Today, Article 4 of the United Nation's Universal Declaration of Human Rights (1948) declares such servitude as illegal; however, neither national nor state legislation have addressed the matter. In America, the Trafficking Victims Protection Act (TVPA) of 2000 extended 'servitude' to cover peonage, or involuntary servitude in payment of a debt.[18])

Slavery was an altogether different matter. Between three and four hundred thousand Africans had arrived in America by 1680.[19] All of them were involuntarily transported to a new continent and held in slavery. Slavery officially ended in America on 18 December 1865 with the adoption of the Thirteenth Amendment to the Constitution. On that date, slavery was lawful only in Delaware, Kentucky, Missouri, Maryland and New Jersey; it had otherwise ended as the result of the Emancipation Proclamation on 1 January 1863 or as a result of changes in the laws of the various states. Since December 1865, the aftermath of slavery has colored, for better or worse and in one way or another, the whole of America history. The writing of local history in the United States is touched by it and the tragedy of slavery is an issue with which each historian should be familiar and must grapple with. Many, many volumes have been written about slavery and its effect on the people, places, and culture of America. The local historian should consult those resources for a full treatment of the subject; they are worth the effort.

Famine

Famine can result from any event, natural or manmade, that disrupts crop growth or the supply chain. A famine is a widespread shortage of food, usually accompanied by regional malnutrition, starvation, epidemic and increased mortality and was an everyday fact in Europe, from 1315 until nearly 1900. Today in America, many people see famine as something that happened in the distant past, or if it happens today, it happens only in unstable Third World countries already ravaged by civil war and political instability. To the European population that came to America, however, famine was no stranger: Europe experienced 39 major famines between 1590 and 1879, lasting a total of twenty years and comprising 20% of the total time period.

In 1315, three years of torrential rains and unpredictable growing season weather ushered in the Great Famine of 1315-1317. Around 1550, glaciers began to expand globally; by 1650 global temperatures dropped 4°-7° C and over the following 200 years, the average temperature of the planet was 4° C colder than it is today.[11] Although English farmers were growing grapes and producing wine for export to France in the late 13th Century, by the 14th Century, those surviving on a feudal farmstead or plot had little chance to avoid starvation.

The Generalized famine in 1590-1600 was the first 'great famine' in Europe since the early 14th Century. It may have resulted, in part from the climatic changes of the Little Ice Age. The only European country not affected was the Netherlands. The Finnish Great Famine of 1696 was probably caused by Little Ice Age as well, but was in part the reason for the Great Famine of Estonia, also known as the Great Starvation.

35

"The Life & Times Of..."

Crops in Estonia began failing in 1694 and 1695, probably due to climate change. Over the succeeding two years, Estonian landlords exported grain to Finland and Sweden, where the crops had failed as well, taking profits while between 70,000 and 75,000 residents of Swedish Estonia died of starvation.

Potato blight was one major cause of famine in Ireland and Scotland between 1845 and 1857. The two famines (1845-1849 in Ireland and 1846-1857 in Scotland) led to the immigration of 1 million Irish and 1.7 million Scots, primarily to the United States.

Figure 1.2 shows a list of the famines that occurred in Europe from the 1315 almost to the beginning of the 20th Century. Some were highly localized but some were continent wide. These periods of famine can be linked to various causes ranging from greed and political policy to volcanic eruption the climatic changes of Little Ice Age, which occurred between about 1500 and about 1700.

DATES	LOCATION AFFECTED
1315-1317	Great Famine of 1315-1317
1590-1600	General Famine in Europe
1601-1603	Russian Famine of 1601; one of the worst famines in all of Russian history; famine killed as many as 100,000 in Moscow and up to one third of Tsar Gudenov's subjects
1611	Anatolia
1618-1648	Famines resulting from the Thirty Years War
1623-1624	England
1636	Spain

1648-1660	Poland; famine resulted from wars, up to one third of the population died
1649	Northern England
1650-1652	Famine in the east of France
1651-1653	Famine throughout much of Ireland during the Cromwellian conquest of Ireland
1661-1662	France
1680	Sardinia
1690	Scotland; 15% of the population died
1693-1694	France; two million deaths resulted
1695-1698	Great Famine of Estonia and Sweden
1696-1697	Finnish Great Famine; one third of population died
1706-1707	France
1708-1711	Prussia; 250,000 deaths (41% of the population)
1709-1710	France
1727-1728	England
1738-1739	France
1740-1741	Ireland
1741	Norway
1750	Spain
1764	Naples
1770-1771	Great Czech Famine; 12% of population died
1771-1772	Saxony and Southern Germany
1773	Sweden
1773	Iceland; 20% of population died; caused by the eruption of the volcano Laki
1788	France: two years previous to the French Revolution saw bad harvests and harsh winters, possibly resulting from strong El Nino cycle or driven by the 1783 eruption of the Icelandic volcano Laki.

"The Life & Times Of..."

1800-1801	Ireland
1811-1812	Madrid; 12,000 deaths
1816-1817	The Year Without A Summer": generalized famine in Europe, probably the result of the 1815 eruption of volcano Tambura
1845-1849	The Great Irish Famine/The Irish Potato Famine; more than 1 million deaths; 1 million refugees fled to the U. S. and Britain as a result of this single event
1846	Northern Portugal
1846-1857	The Highland Potato Famine in Scotland
	Continued from previous page
1866-1868	Finland; 15% of population died
1879	Ireland
1891-1892	Russia; 375,000 to 500,000 deaths

Figure 1.2 European Famines 1590-1900

Some natural events have become so noteworthy as to acquire well-known names, such as the Little Ice Age and the Year Without a Summer.

The Little Ice Age was a major cause of famine in the period from the 14th Century to the middle of the 19th Century. During the Early Medieval period, subsistence farming was what stood between a family and starvation.

The Little Ice Age may have been responsible for two

other events, both in the United States and in the world at large.[12] In 1658, the Swedish army walked across the Great Belt to invade Denmark. In 1780, New York Harbor froze, allowing New Yorkers to walk from Manhattan to Staten Island. In 1608 in London, the Thames froze over and the first of the "Frost Fairs" was held; the last Frost Fair was in 1816, known as "The Year With No Summer." The winter 1777-1778 found George Washington facing the severe weather in Valley Forge, Pennsylvania. During this time, Friedrich Wilhelm Ludolf Gerhard Augustin von Steuben, later known to American history as Baron von Steuben, would train Washington's army to a state of readiness equal to or greater than that of the British Army that opposed it.

The Year Without a Summer was sometimes known as "Eighteen Hundred and Froze to Death." It was one of the names given to to the year 1816, notable because that year demonstrated the power of a one-time occurrence to effect world climate. A year earlier, the eruption of a volcano located in Indonesia, Mount Tambura, caused substantial "nuclear winter-like" climate abnormalities across the American northeast, northern Europe and eastern Canada. It was also, "the last great subsistence crisis in the Western world" according to historian John D. Post.[13]

Plague, Pandemic & Pestilence

Sickness was widespread in Europe until the advent of modern sanitary methods and medicines. Its overall effect on immigration to America is unknown since records of immigration prior to 1894 are scarce, although information is to be found in or inferred from other sources. Sick people were not permitted to board ships simply because of the threat that the crew would become ill. The horror stories of "plague ships," that is, ships where a person with a communicable disease boarded and made all hands ill

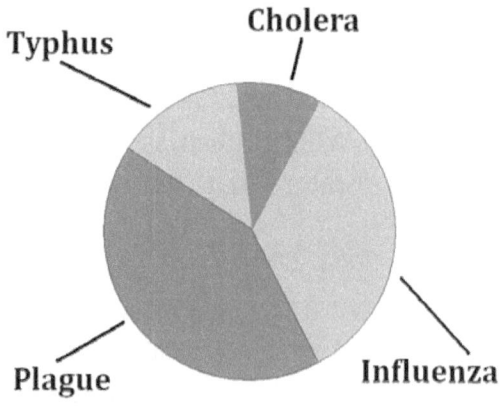

Pandemics, 1381-1831, Europe & Asia: Distribution by Illness

with diseases such as typhoid, typhus, cholera and bubonic plague are many. The suffering of their crews and their treatment in most ports-of-call is well known in the literature and tradition of the sea.[14] This seeming over-cautiousness persists today in shipping; a ship inbound to a port flies the "Q" signal flag to request "free pratique," a clearance from the health authorities of the port.

Widespread sickness was often the norm in Europe, to the

extent that it wasn't noticed by those who were not sick and who were not directly affected by the person or people who were. In the 14th Century, bubonic plague killed between one-third and one half the populations of Europe. Lesser events, usually somewhat more localized, may have killed half the population of some cities, and encouraging flight among healthy citizens.

Bubonic plague was the most persistent and widely distributed of the pandemics afflicting Europe and Asia between 1381 and 1831

Other diseases, some more easily transmitted because of their nature spread with armies and travellers. Figure 1.3 provides a more complete listing.

Years	Disease	Location	Particulars
1348-1349	Plague	Europe	The Black Death; Jews were blamed for causing Plague; Poland was largely spared.
1381-1832	Cholera	Germany	August 1831-from Poland to Berlin; October 1831-Hamburg
1462-1465	Plague	Germany	
1663-1668	Plaque	Europe	
1708-1709	Influenza	Germany	

"The Life & Times Of..."

1738-1740	Plague	Russia	
781-1782	Influenza	Asia and Europe	China to Russia, Poland via Baltic; March-Northern Germany; April-Hungary; May-Austria
788-1789	Influenza	Europe	March 1788
1812-1813	Typhus	Russia	Amongst Napoleon's Army
1812-1814	Typhus	Prussia	
1813-1814	Typhus	Danzig (Gdansk)	Amongst Napoleon's Army
1829-1831	Cholera	Russia	Began in 1826 in India; in 1830
1830-1830	Influenza	Asia and Europe	Began in Asia, in 1830, in Europe 1831
1836-1837	Influenza	Europe	
1361	Plague	Europe	
1371	Plague	Europe	
1382	Plague	Europe	
1602	Plague	Prussia	
1668	Plague	Europe	
1679	Plague	Vienna	
1679	Plague	Vienna	
1709	Plague	Danzig (Gdansk)	June - December (30
1711	Plague	Austria	
1712	Influenza	Germany	April - July

1729	Influenza	Hungary, Poland, Germany	High morbidity
1732	Influenza	Russia, Poland, Germany	
1740	Typhus	Germany	
1742	Influenza	Germany	Spread to Western Europe
1762	Influenza	Europe	Breslau
1807	Typhus	Danzig (Gdansk)	
1813	Typhus	Torgau	
1814	Typhus	Mainz	
1831	Cholera	Galicia	Part of Asiatic Cholera pandemic
1831	Plague	Moldova. Wallachia	Plague merged with Cholera

Figure 1.3 European Pandemics, 1349-1831

War

Western military culture defines war as the "continuation of political intercourse, carried on with other means."[8] It might be a civil war, in which the participants are of a common nationality, or it might be an international dispute characterized orchestrated violence conducted by armies.

Europe was in an almost continuous state of war from about 900 until the end of the Napoleonic Wars in 1815. Figure 1.1 shows the principle European wars during that time.

War is often cited as a driving force behind immigration within Europe, but the effect of war on migration to extra-European colonies was often indirect; from the 13th Century on, medieval kings drew on the middle classes in order to create a military and, later, a bureaucracy that would eventually lay the foundation for royal absolutism of the 16th and 17th centuries.[9] This absolutism became a driving force as it took the form of persecution for religious beliefs and practices, political affiliation, and non-conformist ideas. It set forth policies that caused other calamities, like famine. It also led to a certain amount of immigration during those centuries, particularly where the English Crown sometimes allowed persons who were "difficult" to voluntarily relocate to the Colonies, often to the West Indies or to one of the "company" colonies like Virginia or New England. Once free of the close supervision that resulted from proximity, the immigrants might aspire to the life of a West Indian planter or New England businessman.

War was not the major driving force behind immigration in the early years of American history. War did spark significant immigration in the mid-19th Century. Even so, information on the numbers of immigrants can be sketchy, depending on ship's passenger manifests and family histories. Until the 20th Century, the freedom to travel at will was not universal, and few ship captains would have taken an undocumented traveller aboard simply because of the legal risks to both the ship and the captain. Still, during that time, merchant ship captains were often part-owners of the ships they commanded and money exchanged could result in few or no questions as to the origin of a person.

Since the United States only began to deal with legislation related to immigration after 1870, almost no official records exist for the reasons for immigration to the United States prior to that date and the United States Immigration Service did not exist before 1891. According to the Center for Immigration Studies, in the period from 1900 to 1920, nearly 24 million immigrants arrived during what is known as the "Great Wave." The outbreak of World War I reduced immigration from Europe but mass immigration resumed upon the war's conclusion and Congress responded with a new immigration policy. The national-origins quota system passed in 1921 and revised in 1924. Immigration was limited by assigning each nationality a quota based on its representation in past U.S. census figures. Further, in 1924, Congress created the U.S. Border Patrol within the Immigration Service. Immigration remained low over the next twenty years, dropping below zero for several years and remained low for the twenty years following World War II because of the 1920s era quota system still in use at that time.[10]

Dates	Conflict
	EARLY WAR IN CENTRAL EUROPE
1521-1529	The Ottoman Empire invaded Central Europe; defeated at Vienna.
1530-1556	A religious war, the Peace of Augsburg finally ended war between the Holy Roman Emperor (Charles V) and Protestant nobles.

"The Life & Times Of..."

1740-1748	**WAR OF AUSTRIAN SUCCESSION**
	WAR IN SPAIN AND THE SPANISH NETHERLANDS
1492	Final expulsion of Muslims from of Spain
1566-1609	Revolt in the Spanish Netherlands (The Eighty Years War)
	WAR IN FRANCE
1572-1598	French civil wars. Henry IV issued the Edict of Nantes, which protected the right to practice Protestantism.
1789-1799	French Revolution
	THE ENGLISH CIVIL WARS
1642-1646	First English Civil War
1648-1649	Second English Civil War
	THE NINE YEARS WAR
1688-1697	The Nine Years' War, first of the truly global wars; the Alliance against France was led principally by the Anglo-Dutch King William III (Later, King William I of England), the Holy Roman Emperor Leopold I, King Charles II of Spain and Victor Amadeus, Duke of Savoy
	Continued from previous page
	THE THIRTY YEARS WAR
1618-1648	Holy Roman Emperor Ferdinand II claimed the throne of King of Bohemia. The Bohemians rebelled. Eventually, forces from France, Denmark, Sweden and Spain were involved. In 1640, Portugal revolted and gained its independence from Spain.

1648	The Treaty of Westphalia finally ended the war. France and Spain continued to fight on the seas and in their colonies.
1659	France finally defeated Spain on the seas, leading to the Treaty of the Pyrenees.
	THE HUNDRED YEARS WAR
1337-1453	The House of Valois (French) and the House of Plantagenet (Norman, ruling England) both claimed the French throne. In France, the English invasion, civil wars, deadly epidemics, famines and marauding mercenary armies turned to banditry reduced the population by two-thirds.
	ENGLISH WARS
1689-1815	Second Hundred Years War
1743	War of Austrian Succession
1775-1783	American Revolution
1803-1815	Napoleonic Wars

Figure 1.1 Major European Wars, 1492-1815

(Almost) All of Us Came From Somewhere Else

The immigrants who came to America brought more baggage with them than they could carry: their history, their culture, their beliefs, their religion, and their prejudices. While most of these elements changed or even vanished as the immigrants and their families became Americanized, they were present once and may have had far-reaching (if not immediately apparent) influences on the local or family history, although that influence might not be readily apparent or might be the opposite of that

47

expected.

The effects of a primarily English genesis still abound in the language and general culture of the United States, but they aren't the only effect felt. While the French Quarter in New Orleans has a reputation as a commercial district catering to tourists, most residents will tell anyone who asks that it is, and always has been, a neighborhood, complete with homes, schools, churches, grocery stores, laundries and all the features of any neighborhood in any city. It was planned as a neighborhood and the architecture of the older homes – many of which date from the mid-18th Century – is vaguely reminiscent of France; the settlers sought the familiar. A glance at the street signs gives a hint to the history of the state that's often glossed over: the signs are in English, for the benefit of tourists, but until the early 1990s many were also in French and Spanish as well, discretely recalling the days before the Louisiana Purchase when New Orleans was a French outpost in a Spanish province. These signs reflect history in spite of themselves.

As other groups came to the area, they too built and settled into neighborhoods where the people, the language, the culture and the architecture were familiar. The western boundary of the French Quarter is Canal Street; across Canal Street, the oldest buildings of the English Quarter have an aspect that might have been at home in a larger town in 19th Century England.

In the rural areas of Tennessee, West Virginia and Kentucky, many of the words and expressions heard echo those of Shakespeare, Gray, Chaucer and Alfred the Great. Southern Mountain Dialect, as it's known to linguists, is archaic - not corrupt - English, representing a form heard in the days of Queen Elizabeth I. What is heard today is actually a form associated with Northern England and Scotland. Because of this, even an Anglo-Saxon form appears occasionally.[3] This isn't terribly surprising since the area was settled primarily those known as the Scotch-Irish. The few Palatine Germans who settled in the area left only one linguistic reminder of themselves in the word, *briggety*, which meant, "showing off."[5] As with the street signs of New Orleans, this language – and its writer – is a witness announcing a cultural heritage to the researcher without meaning to. Words and phrases with that "hillbilly" flavor may frequently appear in wills, deeds or other public or private documents of value to the researcher; the writer's use of the Southern Mountain Dialect in a document is a valuable clue in local history.

The effects of America's multicultural beginnings are still felt today. While the majority of Americans claim a British heritage, twenty-five percent of the population of the country lays claim to an African heritage.[6] The second largest Swedish population on Earth is in Chicago. When the scholars of the French *Délégation Générale à la Langue Française* want to study French as it was spoken before it borrowed words from other languages, they travel to southern Louisiana where a 'purer,' older form of French is still spoken as a primary language in many households in places like Lafourche Parish.

In the 19th Century alone, 50 million people left Europe for Americas.[7]

Not All of Us Came From Somewhere Else

Native Americans were here long before the first European appeared on the continent. In many ways, they played an integral part of the settlement of what became the United States. Most of the written historical record about Native Americans began with European contact. Ideologies clashed, old world diseases decimated the native population, religious institutions were challenged, and technologies were exchanged in what would be one of the most devastating meetings of cultures in history.

Native Americans have been cast as the enemy, the friend, and the hero in literature, story, and films. Whatever role they might play in the minds of the American people, they are and always will be the First Americans. Like slavery, the story of the Native Americans is too complex to cover in a single volume and the local historian is encouraged to use the many sources available.

The Past Was Different and Differences Define the Past

In his novel *The Go-Between*, L. P. Hartley wrote that, "The past is a foreign country: they do things differently there." The most fundamental element of a sense of history is this idea: the past was strange and different simply because the passing years have deeply altered the way in which we live. To acknowledge that fact allows the historian to take the measure of that difference and that strangeness. That difference can be seen in the physical manifestations of the past, such as buildings or artifacts, or it may be one of mindset – earlier peoples had values, hopes, fears and attitudes different from our own. Acknowledging and understanding this difference is the essence of historical awareness. Failing to acknowledge that difference, judging the past by our contemporary societal standards is anachronism, the representation of someone or something as existing or happening in other than historical order or context.

So, one of the things a historian aims to do is present the strangeness of the past and present it by placing it in its historical setting – its context – and in so doing, increase the historical awareness of others.

Understanding Historical Context

Seeing these differences as a part of the context of history is critical. An archaeologist would not move an artifact until its physical context was recorded; likewise, the past must be presented in its own contemporary context, rather than that of the historian. Things and events we today see as quaint, cruel, odd, grotesque or disgusting, when presented in the context of it the time and society in which they existed or occurred, are no less shocking or peculiar, but may be explanatory of the nature of that society. *The Hanging Tree*, by V.A.C. Gatrell, was a study of public execution and the English people between 1770 and 1868.

"The Life & Times Of..."

The publisher, Oxford University Press, described it as follows:

> "[Drawn] on letters, diaries, ballads, broadsides, and images, as well as on poignant appeals for mercy which historians until now have barely explored, the book surveys changing attitudes to death and suffering, 'sensibility' and 'sympathy', and demonstrates that the long retreat from public hanging owed less to the growth of a humane sensibility than it did to the development of new methods of punishment and law enforcement, and to polite classes' deepening squeamishness and fear of the scaffold crowd."[20]

Were our relatively recent ancestors more bloodthirsty than we? Were their attitudes reflective of the times, or simply an extension of those learned from their families? *The Hanging Tree* challenges our conventional view of the period, both in England and America, where this same morbid curiosity was transplanted along with the English men and women who colonized the New World. In the American West, hanging was the universally accepted form of capital punishment. Anyone who has ever seen a cowboy movie knows that capital punishment was administered publicly at that time and the citizens gathered around the scaffold to watch the administration of justice. If done improperly, the spectators were treated to the spectacle of a man strangling to death at best or, at worst, to a public decapitation as the victim's head was separated from his body. In early America, as in England, a vast majority of the spectators were women.

If hanging still persists in two of the United States, New Hampshire and Washington,[21] then how different was the past, truly? If one reads *The Prince* with today's sensibilities, it seems, well, Machiavellian. But read through the eyes of a 15th Century Italian man of property and power, it was merely an account of what was right and acceptable. Recent historical research has shown that, by our standards, Vlad the Impaler was a spectacularly cruel man; but as rulers were in Central Europe in the middle 15th Century, when the Ottoman Empire was rolling through the region heaping atrocity upon atrocity, Vlad Dracula was a remarkably restrained king.

Yes, the past was very different.

Recognition of the Historical Process

Understanding of the historical process is implicit in any approach to writing history. The historical process is the synergistic relationship between historical elements or events over time, which makes them – as a group – more significant than they are individually. The relationship between the Treaty of Paris of 1763, the Peace of Paris of 1783, the letter from President Jefferson to his friend, Robert Livingston, in 1802, a 1784 hurricane 200 miles from the Louisiana coast in the Gulf of Mexico and Napoleon's drive to finance a war combine, culminating in the Louisiana Purchase. Related events continued into the 20th Century when a commercial fisherman named Jerry

"The Life & Times Of..."

Murphy snagged one of his nets on an obstruction somewhere south of Mobile Bay; when he finally got the net on deck, he confirmed that yes, the money intended to stabilize the government of New Spain in New Orleans did exist, had been shipped, and all of the 450,000 reales in one-half reales denominations had indeed been lost at sea, which was, until that day, nothing more than unconfirmed rumor.

The local historian should be cognizant of such events and their local effect; however, the local historian should, at the same time, maintain focus on the local aspect of history as defined by the limited geographical area under study even though the methodology for establishing the existence and mechanism of the process is the same for local events as it is for national events.

The above example is from history at a national and international level. While such sweeping events may ultimately have an effect at the local level, it's rare that events in local history will reverberate at the national level. Even so, the local historian must be aware that his or her research may uncover a new or overlooked aspect of history (local or national) that sheds new light on old historical problems. The local historian will be asking questions related to local history, local people and local places and doing research that, because of the historical process, might be equally important.

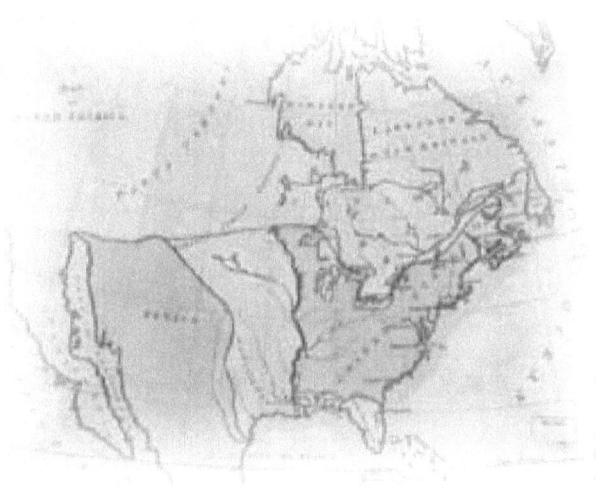

Map of the Louisiana Purchase (Image Courtesy of the National Park Service)

"The Life & Times Of..."

Citations

[1] Evarts Boutell Greene, *The Foundations of American Nationality*, Kessinger Publishing, (2005), p. 1.

[2] Zadock Thompson, History of Vermont: Natural, Civil and Statistical, in Three Parts, with an Appendix, Published by The author, 1853

[3] William Durkee Williamson, The History of the State of Maine: From Its First Discovery, A.D. 1602, to the Separation, A.D. 1820, Inclusive, Glazier, Masters & Co., 1832

4 Richard Hofstadter, Great Issues in American History: From the Revolution to the Civil War, 1765-1865, (Vintage, 1958), p. 220-222. It is suspected, but not certain, that Napoleon saw this letter; in any case, the Louisiana Purchase provided the way to finance his ongoing campaigns in Europe.

5 Wylene P. Dial, "The Dialect of The Appalachian People," West Virginia History, Volume 30, No. 2 (January 1969), pp. 463-71

[6] Center for Immigration Studies, Washington, DC [7] Center for Immigration Studies

[8] Carl von Klauswitz, *On War*, Plain Label Books, 1968. p. 30. Sometimes translated as 'War is the mere continuation of policy by other means.'

[9] Steven Kreis, "Lecture 23: Medieval Society: The Three Orders, Lectures on Ancient and Medieval European History; the author, 2001.

[10] Center for Immigration Studies

[11] S. L. Jaccard, G. H. Haug, D. M. Sigman, T. F. Pedersen, H. R. Thierstein, U. Röhl, "Glacial/Interglacial Changes in Subarctic North Pacific Stratification," *Science* 13 May 2005: Vol. 308. No. 5724, pp. 1003 - 1006

[12] Jaccard, et al., *Ibid*

[13] John D. Post, *The Last Great Subsistence Crisis in the Western World*, Books on Demand, 1977

[14] Some of the most poignant tales can be found in the poetry of Coleridge and Masefield.

[15] William Bradford, Bradford's History "Of Plimoth Plantation" From the Original Manuscript: with a Report of the Proceedings Incident to the Return of the Manuscript to Massachusetts By Massachusetts Office of the Secretary of State, Massachusetts General Court, Wright & Potter printing co., state printers, 1901, p. 14

[16] A reference was located in a life of Mardell Creighton, Bishop of London to the discovery in the library at Fulham Palace of the "MSS known as the Log of the Mayflower" which contains not only the diary of William Bradford (Governor of New Plymouth) but also an authentic register of the births, marriages and deaths of the Colonists of New England from 1620-1650.

The Manuscript was handed over to the American Ambassador in London on 30th April 1897 (Extract from a National Archives Memorandum dated 6 September 1968.)

[17] Roger Daniels, *Coming to America: A History of Immigration and Ethnicity in American Life*, HarperCollins, 2002 p. 30

[18] The United Nations Universal Declaration of Human Rights, adopted and proclaimed by General Assembly resolution 217 A (III) of 10 December 1948

[19] David Eltis, *Economic Growth and the Ending of the Transatlantic Slave Trade*, Oxford University Press (US), 1987

[20] V.A.C. Gatrell, *The Hanging Tree: Execution and the English People 1770-1868*, Oxford University Press, 1996

[21] Death Penalty Information Center, Washington DC. Both states offer lethal injection as an alternative

"The Life & Times Of..."

Chapter 2

Elements of Local History: People, Place ... and Community?

As Geography with History seemeth a carkasse without emotion; so History without Geography wandreth as a Vagrant without a certaine habitation~ - John Smith

While the essential elements of local history are people and place, place is the defining feature. If the study undertaken is local history, the limits are those of the 'local' place, however the local historian may choose to define it.

Limiting the investigation to a specific locale makes the investigative work manageable by decreasing the number of historic elements, records, places, and people associated with its history. Because the scope of the investigation is limited to a very specific geographic area, more in-depth research can be carried out with less chance of confusion.

"The Life & Times Of..."

In family history, place might change with the passage of time as people – the central focus of family history – move from place to place within a locale, a state, or a country. If your interest is in family history, then a single house and its occupants, or a group of related households and the movements and activities of the selected family members through time will supply the limits of the research, whether the place moves across town or across an ocean. If A, A's

Anasazi Ruins, Mesa Verde, Colorado

family, and A's descendents are the subject of the study; and if A immigrated to the United States in 1760, a full family history will include A's early years in the United Kingdom and perhaps his father and grandfather's time there as well.

Simply put, the application of different *types* of geographical limits is a primary difference between family history and local history. The research methods are the same.

America: Urban, Suburban, Rural

Except for cities such as Boston, Philadelphia, New York and Charleston, the population in 18th Century America was scattered between Maine and northern Florida, with diminishing concentrations as one moved away from the cities and inland toward the Alleghenies in the north and the Great Smoky and Blue Ridge Mountains in the south. Only in Pennsylvania had settlers crossed the mountains in any numbers with settlers and traders penetrating the Ohio Valley prior to 1763, into territory ceded to Britain by France in 1763 and known as the Northeast Territory.

For British settlers, the social stratification in much of early America was roughly similar to that with which the settlers were familiar in England, with a significant difference: as in England, there was a ruling class at the top of the social scale and a serving class; in America, however, there was also a "silent class," because of the "peculiar institution" of slavery. By 1760, the population of America was about 1,500,000 persons; about one quarter of them, 275,000, were African slaves. In 1860 those percentages were unchanged.

In the mid-19th Century, Europe was ravaged by civil unrest and revolutionary fervor; in America, Westward expansion played a significant role, causing massive economic growth in the West during the 19th century. The

"The Life & Times Of..."

westward movement of population and the accumulation of productive lands characterized US economic development in the 19th century. In 1848 the Mexican War ended, dumping several thousands of unemployed American soldiers into an expanding job market along with more than a million Europeans who entered the country, migrating to the West following the discovery of gold at Sutter's Creek California that same year. This population brought with them skills that were profitable and not all of them traveled as far as the West Coast. A Welsh hard-rock miner named Morgan Jones saw opportunities in the new technology of the time, the railroad. Rather than incur the expense of building one, he followed the westward expansion of the United States as far as West Texas, developing new methods of construction and maintenance that eventually eased the effort of linking the Atlantic and Pacific coasts. Steamboats traveled the Mississippi, Missouri and Ohio Rivers to destinations in western Pennsylvania, Ohio, Minnesota, and unlikely destinations like Wyoming, revolutionizing the marketing and transportation of goods and lowering the cost to producers.

While the national economy was undergoing substantial change, the regional socio-economic framework was changing as well. Success in the California gold fields turned the national community on its ear almost overnight as doctors, lawyers and businessmen joined the illiterate in the pursuit of an "easy" fortune. It was during this time that the gap between the rich and poor widened and the old classes re-sorted themselves into a seemingly egalitarian society where all were equal but, as George Orwell said of the Animal Farm, "some were more equal than others." It became a society based more on economic than social status as the upper classes of American society were breached by *nouveau riche* characters straight from the mines of California and Colorado. Many people who once associated freely with their neighbors now began to distance themselves, retreating into communities where professionals, storekeepers and clerks would intermingle with those of their own social status.

The escalating industrialization of the mid-19th Century had other effects on communities as well, with the formation of "company towns" where a company provided housing for its workers – usually with rent equaling a substantial portion of their paycheck, leaving just enough to buy minimal food at a company store. One unusual example of this was the Pullman Company.

George Pullman sought to improve relations between management and labor by creating a comfortable community for his workers. He expected them to respond with hard work, and loyalty. The town had landscaped open space, a church and a retail arcade, with everything within walking distance of the factory. By 1893, the population had reached 12,000. There was no local government. A town agent managed the community. The company decided which stores could locate in the town, which books would be stocked in the library, and which performances could be staged at the local playhouse. This lack of a voice in the oversight of the community led to

"The Life & Times Of..."

dissatisfied workers who expressed their discontent frequently, saying that,

> "We are born in a Pullman house, fed from the Pullman shops, taught in the Pullman school, catechized in the Pullman Church, and when we die we'll go to the Pullman Hell."

The community prospered until the depression of 1893. In response to the economic downturn, Pullman reduced wages and hours. He refused to reduce rents or utility prices, even though he was urged to do so by Illinois political leaders. Anger over the financial plight of Pullman workers triggered a bitter 1894 strike against the company. Army troops were called in to quell the. Today, Pullman is nothing more than a Chicago neighborhood.[4]

Another creature of the era was the railroad town. Similar to a company town in that the town was sited was on railroad property and its initial population was railroad workers, often living in tents at first, the railroad town grew beyond the company employees fairly quickly as businesses moved in to take advantage of cheap long term leases of railroad-owned property adjacent to the rights of way, either catering to the railroad workers, or using the railroad to ship their goods.

Company towns generally disappeared by 1930, either through incorporation into municipalities, or by annexation by adjacent cities. The last remaining company towns in America are found in Lake Buena Vista and Bay Lake,

Florida, on land wholly owned by Disney Corporation and populated by a few Disney employees, and in Louisiana, at Pilot Town near the mouth of the Mississippi River, where river pilots have temporary housing during their tour of duty. The permanent population is about 20 and they have their own ZIP Code, 70081.

Regional stratification and sectionalism provoked demographic changes that came into play in other ways. In the South, one out of every ten people lived in cities and towns, where in the north, one out of every three lived in an urban environment. In those southern rural areas, where children were expected to work on the farm from an early age, the average southern white child spent only one-fifth as much time in school as northern counterpart. [1]

Communities formed and split apart during this time of transition. The seeds of political unrest and revolution were beginning to appear as the agrarian South and the industrialized North turned toward head-on collision with the election of Abraham Lincoln in 1860 and the secession from the Union of South Carolina on December 20 of that year.

The Element of Place

"Place" can be defined by geological and vegetative characteristics, or physical changes imposed by the inhabitants, including transportation systems, man-made water systems such as lakes, watersheds, canals, other watercourses or waterways, forestation or political subdivisions and legal boundaries.

The legal boundaries of a place often define the limits wherein government can exercise its rights and authority, provide services to the public and to collect taxes in an area.

The boundaries of political subdivisions of an area are the second most readily recognized geographic limits, the most recognizable being the topographic and geophysical characteristics of an area. In the United States, the most familiar are:

Lot, Subdivision: All county record offices usually have a complete record of owners and occupants, dating from the first recorded sale of the land.

Frequently, individual lots and subdivided parcels are described on the deeds using a system called "metes and bounds." This type of legal description is that used by land surveyors. Frequently the terms subdivision and neighborhood are interchangeable.

Neighborhood: Most neighbourhoods begin their official existence with a 'plat' of land to be subdivided by a developer. Some develop around a single pre-existing home when the owner decides to sell some of their land; other as a family's children build their own homes on a portion of the family's land.

In the first case, the county records office will provide the best information. In the second case, it may be necessary

The Elements of Local History

to go to the County Tax Offices, since improvements built by the family may not require a subdivision of the land, but the improvements will change the tax assessment and will appear of record.

Village, Town or City: A town or city may be a group of neighbourhoods, or a single business district with a few houses. In either case, it's the smallest political subdivision that has the power to pass enforceable local law, appoint law enforcement officers, and conduct court.

Parish: In some parts of the South, it's based on the parishes or former parishes of the Anglican Church. In this case, a county may have one or more parishes. In Louisiana, a parish is the equivalent of a county, probably based on parishes or former parishes of the Catholic Church.

Metropolitan Area: Metropolitan areas consist of at least one large city; many include the "bedroom communities" sharing a boundary with the city and may be part of more than one county or parish.

Cities and metropolitan areas may also include limited political subdivisions, such as special taxation or other "districts" or "authorities" created to serve a specialized purpose or use, such as the provision of public transportation, and may or may not have a physical existence. The district represents the limits of a city's ability to levy taxes to support the specialized purpose, as in the case of the Denver Regional Transportation District (public transit) or the Metropolitan Atlanta Rapid Transit Authority.

County: The largest political subdivision of a state, which may be larger or smaller than a metropolitan area. Charleston, South Carolina, lies entirely within Charleston County; New Orleans, Louisiana, encompasses all or part of seven parishes, the Louisiana equivalent of a county.

National Boundaries: The legal limits of a country's physical land area. The legal limits of a country's authority may extend beyond its national boundaries, as in an Exclusive Economic Zone at sea, or on land in the form of colonies, protectorates, or territories.

Boundaries so can completely define a place that among the questions that the local historian must address are those concerning the ways that the presence or absence of a legal or physical boundary would obstruct or promote human occupancy.

**Manmade Features,
Structures & Urban Planning**

Whether a county road or city street that began life as an animal trace through the wilderness, or an interstate highway that was once a wagon or cattle drive trail between towns, roads can express boundaries and determine growth within inhabited places.

A road in a given location insures that, consistent with other geographical and geological limitations and questions of ownership of adjacent and nearby property, housing will appear and other businesses and services will locate along or near the alignment. Placement and the alignment of roads within an area will affect population presence and growth and density along the road, establish neighborhood limits and define the physical limits of a community or lead to the establishment of new communities.

It would be a mistake to assume that most roads and streets, particularly in an urban environment, began their existence as wild animal tracks. Urban planning – the design of communities to best use the natural features in an organized manner – is generally deemed to have taken on its modern form in Greece in the 5th Century BCE, although Egyptian and Mesopotamian cities as well as those in the Indus Valley, were carefully designed in a grid pattern in the third millennium BCE. While many of the older cities on the both coasts of the United States may have large areas that have been intensively designed, these areas are usually less than a century old (Washington, DC is a spectacular exception). Still, in general terms it is likely that, even if the original "Main Street" was a relatively straight stretch of an animal track, an informal grid pattern developed to either side of Main Street as the town developed. How did urban planning affect the early community?

Today, urban planning takes the commercial needs of the populace, safety, transportation, and aesthetics into consideration as well as the natural terrain and environment of the area. The development of zoning and subdivision ordinances has tended to make mixed use environments – where a stockyard might be located between two homes, or a home might be located in the middle of the central business district of Main Street – a thing of the past. Zoning ordinances are one of the legal tools which cities or counties control land use and growth. They are the means by which planners implement the "vision" of the city's government for its growth, development and land use. If older plans are available, they constitute either a primary or a secondary historical source, documenting changes in the uses permitted within a geographically delimited area that may provide a benchmark from which to commence a search regarding the former activities within a location. Note that zoning ordinances will document land uses permitted by right (those which are inherent in ownership) and may include prescriptive uses – those permitted either by law or by a variance specific to a property – or descriptive uses, those which have a historic basis.

Zoning ordinances may also detail specific and forbidden uses, which may offer an insight into the historic use of a location.

The regulations, therefore, become an unwitting witness providing testimony as to the facts of local history, as do the documents associated with any effort of the planning effort. Consequently, The indirect impact of recent urban planning efforts on local history is more one of organization of information, past and present, including both contemporary and past zoning ordinances.

Another impact is historic Preservation and the establishment, in many towns, cities and counties is the development of specific zoning to protect or adaptively re-use historic buildings and locations. Sources may be available including:

- Documentation of physical condition and changes made; may be in the form of an investigative or archaeological report;

- Documentation of changes in use, including renovation or restoration of buildings and adaptive re-use of older buildings or of space formerly occupied by older buildings which were not salvageable - if a building is demolished and its location is converted to green space, there may be an archaeological investigation of the location and records of any evidence recovered.

Transportation systems in an area are also such a witness. When was a road first paved, and by whom, and why? When was an airport built? Railroads have much the same affect as other transportation components, except that construction, operating costs and the physical constraints of operation – the train has to stay on the track - make the railroad less flexible. Adaptive reuse of railroad rights-of-way is now common and may influence conclusions in local history. Railroads have the added advantage (to the historian) of being heavily documented.

Adequate, proper research requires the local historian question the presence and level of development of transportation in a place, seeking to determine how or if transportation had an effect on the occupancy of a place and, if so, to what extent.

Natural features

Natural features include waterways and watercourses, cliffs, hills, rises, berms, soil characteristics and types, depth of bedrock, forestation and availability of timber, and exposure to sunlight and weather.

When considering place, each of these characteristics leads to questions about when, why and how people settled in a particular location. Associated with these are questions such as, was water easily accessible, was the ground too stony to farm, was the area stable enough to build on and was there sufficient sunlight for growing food? Was timber available to build with or to use for firewood and were there trees for windbreaks? Was the area defensible against natural predators and human attack? The answer to each of these questions represents an impact that place has on people. These questions may also answer other questions about how people changed the landscape to suit their needs; one quick, practical means of determining the way people changed the place is checking old maps, which are usually easily available online. Another is to check county records.

You can also look at the building materials used: in the

early years of Winfield, Kansas, the area was known to have large stands of walnut and bull pine trees. The older homes there are, by and large, made of walnut planking or have walnut sheathing under the brick or pine exterior. Interior finishes may appear to be oak, but are actually walnut or bull pine, painted to resemble the grain of oak or another wood. Furniture made in the region in the 19th Century is generally walnut and the original stains used on the furniture were made from walnut sap, which turned the wood almost black.

The question for the historian is, are these buildings, their manner of construction and materials, and their grounds and outbuildings, giving subtle testimony to the local history?

The People

Discovering the people who lived within an area is more complex than establishing their identities. It's exploring their way of life (within, as always, the proper historical context), their employment, their amusements, their spirituality, their worldview, and their associations and links with their neighbours and the larger world.

Simple curiosity brings several questions to mind, usually in the pattern of "who, what, where, when, why, and how," the classic questions of the reporter: who settled here, what did they find here that made settlement in this location worthwhile? Where did they come from and why? How did they arrive? These are the questions that both the local

"The Life & Times Of..."

and the family historian must ask.

In the early days of America, patterns of settlement were generally established by the sponsors of the various colonies, such as the London & Virginia Company, in the case of Virginia and New England and the Dutch West India Company, which founded New Netherland. Society was stratified much as it had been before coming to the new continent, and that stratification prevailed for varying periods of time according to the racial, ethnic, religious, or social status of the group or subgroup of the population and further, according to the region and location. The beginnings of upward mobility for many groups did not appear until after the late 19th Century, when women, minorities, and workers began to gain a voice and to avoid what historian E. P. Thompson called, "the enormous condescension of history."[4]

"At Fifty-sixth and Lexington Avenue, the women voters showed no ignorance or trepidation, but cast their ballots in a businesslike way that bespoke study of suffrage." (Courtesy of the Library of Congress)

Some of the initial settlers in America were clergy or military men (even those described as "adventurers" had military experience). Some were hired colonists, paid to stay with a colony for a period of time. The majority represented a cross-section of English society: coopers, merchants, weavers, farmers, printers, doctors, merchants, blacksmiths and an undertaker. The manifest of the Mayflower lists several indentured servants and a maid. One passenger was noted as being a wealthy separatist, another, only six years old at the time, was of royal descent and a member of the gentry.

Researching a community in early America may involve researching not only the "main community" in a place, but also a wide variety of "sub-communities," simply because of the social demarcations that existed in early American society owing to the presence of slaves, indentured servants and nuclear families within and amongst all these groups.

Community as a Separate Entity

While acknowledging that local history has two essential elements, People and Place, the two combine to form a separate entity, Community.

In sociology, the concept of community is the subject of endless debate, and the sociologists are yet to reach agreement on a definition of the term. One can find 94 discrete definitions of the term as early as mid-1950s, implying that the concept of community is intuitive rather than definitive. Traditionally a "community" has been defined as a group of interacting people living in a

"The Life & Times Of..."

common location. The word is often used to mean a group that is organised around common values and social cohesion within a shared geographical location, generally in social units larger than a household.

Gregory Gold Diggings, Colorado May 1859 (Image Courtesy of the Library of Congress)

Many factors influenced the formation of communities in early America. In addition to the terrain and landscape of place, numerous social factors came into play. Common ethnicity, national origin, language, and religion, leads the list of reasons for the existence of a community in early America as a living entity. Obligations, local governance, employment or membership in guilds or unions, worldview, health, or prejudices – either within the community or external to the community, all contributed to the formation of community in a group of people within a single location.

Quite naturally, people within a limited geographic location usually have common relationships to some degree. Communities may be "thick" communities, consisting a people who share a wide range of characteristics, or "thin" communities, where the members only share a very few. Any discussion of people in history, and particularly local history, must recognize both people and the network of relationships within a place, making community the essential synthesis of People and Place.

The interactions between the people would include those of familial associations, those by birth or kinship, are the earliest and simplest form of community. The community formed by family will likely extend beyond the physical boundaries of the local historian's research. Professional or employment relationships may be nearly as strong as familial relationships and may also extend beyond the boundaries of the local physical community, with implications far beyond that of employment.

Ethnicity, that is, a common cultural, racial or religious background is often cited as the reason social communities formed within geographic communities. One example of an ethnic community forming within a larger geographic community can be found in the archetypal antebellum plantation in the South. The plantation was as self-sufficient and independent as a feudal manor, a community

"The Life & Times Of..."

in its own right, with specialists in every skill necessary to the efficient operation of a farm, from woodworkers to metalworkers, ferriers, farm hands and blacksmiths. The community within this plantation community was an ethnic community, held in slavery, but a community nonetheless, sharing a common racial heritage, in many cases a common religion or religions, and the experience of chattel slavery. This community within a community required its own support system of cooks, medical and service personnel; in addition, this community provided the general support system for the people who occupied "the big house" as well, in the form of farm labour and household functionaries. One central aspect of community that sociologists acknowledge is that *the community must be aware of itself as a community*. Without social awareness and cohesion, what would otherwise be a community is merely a group of people living in a common location, perhaps with some interaction, but with none of the interrelationships inherent in the concept of community, nor the single voice that community implies.

If community is the synthesis of people and place, it deserves the same historical scrutiny as people and place. The same questions of, "who, what, where, when, why, and how" should be applied; a family historian might research a single individual or a single family group within a place, but if the family historian – and the local historian, as well – expands their investigation to include the community as a whole, they will realize that, not only did the people affect the landscape, but the affected each other as well. By discovering how, what, why and when the community acted on the individual lives of its members and how those people acted to change both themselves and their community, we can expand our knowledge of the local history of the area.

Adding to the Mix: The Effects of Transplanted Regionalism on Local History

While America, as was stated earlier, might be the child of Europe, America is significantly larger than Europe which gives rise to a unique form of an egalitarianism resulting from freedom of movement throughout the large and diverse landscape of America without constraints such as an internal passport.

Even in the years of European colonial presence on the Eastern shores of continent, the second and succeeding generations of Americans were curious about what was over the next hill or beyond the next valley and the westward expansion of country. Early settlement in Tennessee, Kentucky and the Ohio Valley were the result of this curiosity and need for lands necessary to accommodate a growing population.

Manifest Destiny,[2] originally a political rallying cry, became the watchword for this expansion of America from the Atlantic seaboard to the Pacific coast. The political aspect was overshadowed as such events as the California Gold Rush of 1849 led to widespread settlement across the continent and the formation of new Territories and, eventually, states. The transcontinental telegraph in 1861 and the transcontinental railroad in 1869 rapidly added new elements to communication and travel with locations so far distant from the original American settlements that the original cultures that accompanied those who migrated west had no time to disappear as new regional attitudes and manners developed from variety of cultural inputs imposed on a localized area took hold and grew alongside them: Victorian Italianate homes in Kansas look little different in their physical design from their counterparts in San Francisco, but in San Francisco, the homes were wearing brighter colors and acquired the title of "Painted Ladies."

This great internal migration from the Atlantic coast continued well into the 19th Century and saw the development of pockets ethnic conformity within a larger social setting, like Swedish and Dutch neighborhoods in Chicago and neighborhoods with a distinctly Asian character in the western United States.

Communities Resulting from Racial, Religious, and Other Social Prejudices In America

The slave communities that developed and grew within the confines of southern plantations were uprooted by war and freedom, and "free slave" communities, such as those that still exist on the South Carolina and Georgia Sea Islands still preserve unique characteristics of community that were known by their ancestors, along with history, religion, tradition and manners of their past. They have also preserved the language known as Gullah.

Predominantly black communities later grew on the fringes of mainstream America. The narrator in Ralph Ellison's novel, *The Invisible Man*, tells of growing up in a black community in the South. The story is both frightening and compelling and speaks to such a local history unlike any other book.

Prejudices played a large part in the development of America; they held the country back for many, many years and, when they were addressed, and were judged in the court of public opinion and the community – as most things surely are judged – those prejudices faltered and

Manzanar War Relocation Center, 1943 (Photo by Ansel Adams, Courtesy of the Library of Congress)

began to be replaced with a new sense of clarity, although that sense of clarity sometimes blurred. The shocking images and descriptions of slavery were replaced by other images and descriptions of prejudice in America a scant 75 years later:

> "After Japan bombed Pearl Harbor on December 7, 1941, fear of a Japanese invasion and subversive acts by Japanese-Americans prompted President Franklin D. Roosevelt to sign Executive Order 9066 on February 19, 1942. The act designated the West Coast as a military zone from which "any or all persons may be excluded." Although not specified in the order, Japanese-Americans were singled out for evacuation. More than 110,000 people of Japanese ancestry were removed from their homes in California, southern Arizona, and western Washington and Oregon and sent to ten relocation camps."[3]

Even after the Emancipation Proclamation and the changes to the Constitution to make all men and women free and equal before the law, the early years of World War II gave us images of 110,000 Americans of Japanese ancestry incarcerated in "relocation camps." These same years saw the U.S. Army's 442nd Regimental Combat Team, composed almost completely of Nisei, the sons of those Japanese immigrants, all American citizens, fighting in Europe, where they won or were awarded:

- 52 Distinguished Service Crosses, 19 of which were later upgraded to Medals of Honor,
- 1 Distinguished Service Medal,
- 588 Silver Stars,
- 22 Legion of Merit Medals,
- 15 Soldier's Medals,
- 5,200 Bronze Stars, 1 of which was later upgraded

to a Medal of Honor, *and*
- 9,486 Purple Hearts.
- Twenty-one members of the 442nd were awarded the Congressional Medal of Honor, America's highest honor for heroism above and beyond the call of duty in combat.

The 442nd is the most highly decorated unit in U.S. Military history.

As the madness of war passed with the dawn of a Nuclear Age, the old attitudes were diluted in form through the years until finally, in the years following the passage of the Civil Rights Act of 1964 the memory of those old ways and prejudices diminished, nearly fading from the public consciousness.

The local historian should never forget that these oppressed communities are part of history and contributed to the whole. Neither they, nor their contributions, should be forgotten or ignored.

"The Life & Times Of..."

Citations

Ralph Ellison, *The Invisible Man*, Modern Library, 1994

Geneviève Fabre, Robert G. O'Meally, *History and Memory in African-American Culture*, Oxford University Press, 1994

Donna L. Franklin, William Julius Wilson, *Ensuring Inequality: The Structural Transformation of the African-American Family*, Oxford University Press US, 1997

Karen V. Hansen, Anita Ilta Garey, *Families in the U.S.: Kinship and Domestic Politics*, Temple University Press, 1998, ISBN 1566395909, 9781566395908

[1] U. S. Census of Population and Housing, U. S. Bureau of the Census, 1860.

[2] The phrase was used originally by Jacksonian Democrats in the 1840s to promote the political annexation of the Oregon Territory, Texas and the areas in the American Southwest known as the Mexican Cessession.

[3] These comments are found in the Prints & Photographs Catalogue of the Library of Congress, concerning the Ansel Adams photographs of WWII relocation camps.

[4] Edward P. Thompson, "The Making of the English Working Class," *Journal of Social History*, Volume 1, No. 3 (Spring 1968), pp. 288-294.

"Manzanar War Relocation Center, Winter 1943" Library of Congress, Prints & Photographs Division, Ansel Adams, photographer, [reproduction number, e.g., LC-A35-4-M-56]

4 William H. Carwardine, The Pullman Stike: The Classic First-Hand Account of an Epoch-Making Struggle in US Labor History, Charles Kerr, 1994

The Elements of Local History

"The Life & Times Of..."

Chapter 3

Beginning to Do History: Sources, Questions and the Historical Method

Skepticism is history's bedfellow – Edgar Saltus

If you want to explore a foreign county, your journey begins long before you leave your home. You order brochures, and do research on the Internet; you go to the local library to get books on the culture, the cities, and geography. You get copies of newspapers from the country and ask people who've been there. In other words, you'd acquire as many sources of information about that country as possible.

Historical research is little different.

Beginning to Do History: Historical Sources

Historical sources are any source of historical information. Historical sources include records of birth and of death, marriage and divorce, the purchase of a home and land, legal actions, and military service. They may include letters, diaries, a local book of local history, a newspaper, government documents, reports or photos of any sort or artifacts recovered from the filled-in pits of privies. Sometimes, sources may be what historian Marc Bloch called "unwitting witnesses" to history: a play, a movie, an audio file or track that contains some element that provides historical information without having been intended to do so.

Historical Sources

Historical sources are divided into three broad categories, generally on the basis of how near they were to the event or incident, if they are original, and whether they include comments on the incident, or are simply references which point to other documents.

Primary sources are original sources; documents, recordings or other sources of information that were created at the time being studied, by an authoritative source, usually one with direct personal knowledge of the events being described. A primary source is a source that is not based on any other existing or kept source.

Secondary sources are generally those that describe and

interpret original research from primary sources. One example might be a history text or a book like Decline and Fall of the Roman Empire, by the historian Edward Gibbon. Another might be the History of White County, Tennessee, by the Rev. Monroe Seals. Secondary sources include books and monographs, published or unpublished, on county history, town history up to a specified date, usually the date of publication. In the case of the family historian, secondary sources might include books, genealogies previously prepared or monographs which detail the history of a family up to a certain date. The line between primary and secondary sources may seem blurred at times; a primary source may be a replacement of a lost source – a copy, designated as a replacement may be considered a primary source. Of course, should the "lost" document be found, the copy becomes a secondary source.

Secondary sources are where the local historian should begin investigating local history. They are usually available at local libraries, museums and through historical societies. One of the greatest advantages of beginning your research with a secondary source is that the historical emphasis of an older work, even if it's only twenty or thirty years old, may be different. New facts may have come to light that point to a different direction for investigation, or discrepancies between fact and "history" may have become more apparent, begging for further research by the local historian. While a secondary source may seem to avoid the "re-invention of the wheel, some secondary sources may conflict on a few – or many – points. Original sources should be checked if at all possible. Many original sources are available on the Internet. Resources such as those found at the National Archives and Records Administration or the National Archives of the United Kingdom are priceless and are either freely available or available at a very low cost.

Almost all secondary sources are available from retail sources or they may be freely available on the Internet, through sources such as Google Books. In many cases, their authors have done much of the difficult work of translating and transcribing old documents or have included references that point the way to original documents. In some cases, they even include copies of the original document.

Primary and secondary sources can also include literary works, novels or plays in which the playwright or novelist describes "things as they were," simply because they must: the audience knew what to expect in the way of speech, scenery, and behavior, and would not believe anything else. Therefore, not only is William Shakespeare's work a testimonial to the language of the time of Elizabeth I, it also inadvertently discloses much information about the attitudes of his contemporaries to such diverse subjects as death, life, wealth or lack of wealth, religious prejudices of the time, and a myriad of other ideas, methods, technologies, religion, work and worldview, thus making the Bard of Avon an "unwitting witness to history."

Tertiary sources can come in any one of four forms. They might be a list of primary and secondary resources, they might be an index or compilation of citations and include directions for the use of secondary sources, they might be digests of secondary source information or they might also be sources, which are once removed in time from secondary sources.

Tertiary sources provide the local and family historian with another potential starting point, but on a broader basis. Many online sources can be found, such as the Aussie Educator website, where primary and secondary resources of the English Institute for Historical Research are readily available.

Understanding the nature of historical resources is only the first step in the journey. The next step is determining the credibility of the resource.

Credibility of the Historical Source: Critical Thinking

We usually expect "historical" resources to be correct, accurate, fair, unbiased and without the prejudices of propaganda, self-deception, distortion or misinformation. However, historical documentation can be rife with any or all of those characteristics: history can indeed be based on a true story.

The Nature of Sources

Any historical resource, whether primary, secondary or tertiary, may reflect all the elements mentioned above, for any number of reasons. Perhaps a diary was altered or had pages removed to avoid having to explain "uncomfortable" circumstances, or an official report was prepared in a certain way – ignoring facts that were unpleasant, or simply inconvenient – in order to avoid official censure. Perhaps the writer or speaker was so heavily influenced by their own feelings that they believed they had presented the truth objectively while, in fact, they had not.

As an example, ship's logs from the Battle of Trafalgar in 1805 carry accounts of the Battle so prejudiced by nationalism and so clouded by the fog of war that, were you not able to plot the individual ships position on a nautical chart on the date in question and at the appropriate time, you might think that each ship's captain was describing an entirely different event. Even the Command Logs of the combined French and Spanish fleets suffer from the same hints of self-deception and distortion, as this French dispatch reveals:

> "Head Quarters, Cadiz, Oct. 25
>
> The operations of the Imperial Navy mirror in the Atlantic those of the grand Imperial Army in Germany.
>
> The English fleet is annihilated - Nelson is no more. Indignant at being inactive in Port, while our brave brothers in arms were gaining laurels in Germany, Admirals Villeneuve and Gravina resolved to put to sea and give the English a fight. They were superior in number, 45 to our 33, but

what is that, to men determined to fight and win. Nelson did everything to avoid a battle, he attempted to enter the Mediterranean but we chased him, and caught him off Trafalgar. The French and Spaniards vied with each other to get into action first. Admiral's Villeneuve and Gravina were both anxious to lay their ships alongside the Victory, the English Admiral's ship. Fortune, so constant always to the Emperor, did not favor either of them - the Santissima Trinidad was the fortunate ship. In vain did the English Admiral try to avoid action but the Spanish Admiral Oliva prevented his escape, and lashed his vessel to the English flagship. The English ship was one of 186 guns; the Santissima Trinidad was but a 74. Lord Nelson adopted a new system, afraid of meeting us in the old way, in which he knows we have superiority of skill, as we proved by our victory over Sir Robert Calder. He attempted a new mode of fighting. For a short time he confused us, but what can confuse his Imperial Majesty's navy for long?"

While this is a blatant example of the taint of politics and self-interest, even the most innocuous sources must be evaluated critically.

That "taint of politics" can be found in many official documents. Before you think that it renders the document invalid, consider that the "taint" is, in itself, an unwitting witness to history, reflective of not only the attitude of the writer, but perhaps a wider attitude as well.

The Characteristics of Sources

One of the most important characteristics of any source is its provenance. Provenance, from the French *provenir*, "to come from," means the origin or source, of something, or the history of the ownership or location of an object. In archival practice, proof of provenance is provided by the operation of control systems that document the history of records kept in archives, including details of amendments made to them. Provenance is also one of the most important aspects of a historical source. It has six elements: date, localization, authorship, analysis, integrity and credibility, all of which are form the guidelines for critical thinking.

In *A Guide to Historical Method*, historian Gilbert J. Garraghan summarizes critical thinking in six questions:

1. *When* was the source, written or unwritten, produced (date)?
2. *Where* was it produced (localization)?
3. By *whom* was it produced (authorship)?
4. From what *pre-existing material* was it produced (analysis)?
5. In what *original form* was it produced (integrity)?
6. *What is* the evidential value of its contents (credibility)?[1]

Do the questions look familiar?

The first four (*when, where, who, how/why*) are classified as higher criticism. Higher criticism focuses on the origins of a document to determine who wrote it, when it was written, and where.

The fifth query *(what)* is lower criticism. Lower criticism focuses on potential errors in the text of the source such as those resulting from re-copying or poor memory. It attempts to determine the original form and wording of a document no longer extant, or extant in a language not native to the local area; for example a land grant in Spanish. It's primarily concerned with determining an accurate text in cases where we have copies instead of the original.

The first five queries represent *external criticism*, using the external characteristics of the source to determine its authenticity and provenance of a source. Query 6 is an *internal* criticism of the source. As Louis Gottschalk pointed out in *Understanding History*, few documents are accepted as completely reliable, setting down the general rule that, "For each particular of a document the process of establishing credibility should be separately undertaken regardless of the general credibility of the author."[2] An author's trustworthiness may, in the main, establish a probability for the consideration of each statement, but each part of each piece of evidence extracted must be weighed individually.

When was the source created? Knowing the provenance of a document, when was written, when an oral history was taken and under what circumstances, or when a photograph, painting, drawing or map was made is essential to any effort in local or family history.

Where did the historical resource originate? Did it come from a government archive or a private source? Often, information received from private sources, such as copies of letters or diaries, may have been edited either by the original writer in an attempt to avoid later- and embarrassing – difficulties or by a later hand trying to explain away unpleasant circumstances. Is the subject of the document or interview out of place? A discussion of whales beached on the banks of the Mississippi River may seem so out of place as to be ridiculous and, in all probability it would be. However, it has been known to happen – in southern Louisiana, near the river's mouth. If the resource appears "out of place" without explanation, it needs to be inspected further and outside confirmation of its veracity sought. An example of this involves recently discovered documents in the National Archives of the United Kingdom, that established the existence a French eyewitness to the Battle of Trafalgar whose log, as a helmsman, confirmed certain aspects of French activities. The documents had been "missing" because paperwork had been misfiled more than a hundred years ago. Because it was found in the wrong place, a long and substantial effort was expended to prove the provenance of the document successfully.

"Where did it originate?" In the case of the missing French account of Trafalgar, the provenance and not the physical location was part of the document's pedigree. As it turned out, the document was filed with other paperwork related to the battle.

"Who created the source? Were they a witness to an event? Were they a participant? Did they have first hand knowledge or did they simply report or record the event?" Written in French, the author was a helmsman in the French fleet. While he reported the event indirectly as part of a log, he was a participant, a key distinction between a primary and secondary source, and one that helps to establish the source's provenance.

Garraghan's fourth query, *from what pre-existing material was it produced,* is directed at secondary sources, those produced after the fact from original sources. Historian R.J. Shafer concurs with Garraghan's method, concluding that higher criticism included "Determination of authorship and date involves one or all of the following: (a) content analysis, (b) comparison with the content of other evidence, (c) tests of the physical properties of the evidence." Content analysis includes examinations of anachronisms in language, datable references, and consistency with a cultural setting. Comparison with other writings may involve palaeography, the study of the style of handwriting, the study of stylometry and comparison of literary style with known authors, or something as simple as a reference to the document's author in another one of his works or by a contemporary. Physical properties

101

include the properties of the paper, the consistency of the ink, and the appearance of a seal, as well as the results of radioactive carbon dating.

The fifth query, *in what original form was it produced*, is called "lower criticism," Approaches to this form of criticism include eclecticism, stemmatics, and cladistics. At the heart of eclecticism is the idea that one should adopt the reading as original, that most easily explains the derivation of the alternative readings. Stemmatics attempts to construct a "family tree" of extant manuscripts to help determine the correct reading. Cladistics makes use of statistical analysis in a similar endeavor.

The sixth query, which concerns the *evidential value of the source*, makes two qualifications to the historian: first, is it related to the research being undertaken? Second, is it real? Is it a document? Artifact? Oral Tradition? Oral history? Never forget that all can be forged or faked. The Piltdown Man had scientists baffled until 1953.

Two special categories of source, eyewitness testimony (or eyewitness evidence) and oral history, require special handling when used as source material.

Eyewitness Evidence

Eyewitness evidence presents special problems because of the potential for both misinterpretation and untruthfulness, either by error or by design.

The missing French document described above is an

example. It's a helmsman's log of the steering orders aboard the French ship *Mont Blanc*, which participated in the battle. Because of the nature of the document – one of the vessel's *internal* logbooks, rather than a personal narrative – it can reasonably be assumed that the account of the ship's actions that it contains is an accurate account of the battle from the French perspective by a participant. A statement by an eyewitness has meaning, but is the real meaning of the statement different from its literal meaning? Two possibilities come to mind with that question, the first being that the statement was ironic in nature and the second, that the words used in the statement were used in an archaic manner: the past was different, so were the meanings of many words, even some we use today.

Another set of questions for eyewitness evidence would begin with, "How well could the person making the statement observe the thing that he is reporting? Was his physical situation such that he could properly observe? Did he understand the languages in play, or have the expertise to understand what was transpiring? Was he able to freely observe without threat or intimidation?" In the case of the helmsman's log from the Battle of Trafalgar, the helmsman was in a unique position to observe the action aboard the *Mont Blanc* freely and without threat and, as he was recording the steering orders, not only must he have understood the language in which the orders were issued, but he was required to (1) repeat the helm order back to the officer issuing it and then execute the order, and (2) recorded the order in the helm log. As the helmsman, in

103

charge of steering the ship in a battle, he was, of necessity, an expert at his assigned job.

Questions about the timing of the source's preparation need to be answered in order to assess validity. Was there any indication that he was prejudiced regarding the matter at hand? Was his report made in haste, or was it done in a thoughtful manner? Was the statement/document prepared in a timely manner? Was his statement prepared soon after the event, or much later? In the case of the *Mont Blanc*'s helmsman's log, questions of prejudice regarding the matter at hand evaporate because of the nature of the document: any vessel log, whether the captain's log with which most people are familiar or the speed log, helm log or bell book, all are part of the documentation by which the vessel is navigated, whether in crossing an ocean or pulling away from a pier and out of dock. As such, the lives of all aboard depend on their being as accurate as possible, without prejudice, inaccuracy or the taint of politics.

Was the log prepared in haste? Even in battle, the movements of a sailing ship are ponderous at best. During the Battle of Trafalgar, most ships achieved a top speed of less than seven miles per hour and, since the logs were used in the decision making process for planning sailing maneuvers, the logs were carefully, deliberately kept in a timely manner at the time the steering orders were given.

A Test of Judgment

The eyewitness made a report, sometime, about something that may have been observed properly or improperly. Why? Why did this person take the time to make a report? What was his intention in reporting whatever it was? More importantly, to whom and for whom did he report? If he was acting on behalf of a third party, would that third party be likely to ask him to "distort" the facts of the matter? Would they go so far as to suggest a distortion?

Did the statement have a quality of JDLR ("Just Don't Look Right")? Are there any indications of, or clues that hint at the veracity of the statement? Was the statement indifferent in its tone, making distortion unlikely? Did the statement include information damaging or incriminating to the eyewitness, indicating that he was not seeking to distort the truth? Was casual information included that was not intended to mislead? If the JDLR factor is high, then the statement probably contains at least some element of untruth.

Discrediting Eyewitness Evidence
As a Test of Its Validity

Some types of information are easier to observe and report than others. Wild claims of sea serpents in Scottish lakes notwithstanding, do the witness's statements conflict with what we accept as reality? If they're contrary to human nature, is there a plausible explanation?

Finally, are there internal conflicts in the evidence that impeach the witness's own testimony?

Any attorney will tell you that a witness's credibility is only as great as his ability to resist being impeached – in less generous terms, can the witness be caught in a lie? If not in a lie, then can the witness be caught contradicting his own testimony?

Any policeman will tell you that a witness's credibility can only be measured by taking one half of what they say as being half-true: a witness is caught up in the moment; if the moment is stressful, joyful, or startling, or if the witness is hungry, angry, lonely or tired, those emotions or those feelings will have a diminishing effect on the credibility of their statement. See JDLR, above.

Historian Louis Gottschalk adds an additional consideration:

> Even when the fact in question may not be well-known, certain kinds of statements are both incidental and probable to such a degree that error or falsehood seems unlikely. If an ancient inscription on a road tells us that a certain proconsul built that road while Augustus was princeps, it may be doubted without further corroboration that that proconsul really built the road, but would be harder to doubt that the road was built during the principate of Augusutus. If an advertisement informs readers that 'A and B

Coffee may be bought at any reliable grocer's at the unusual price of fifty cents a pound,' all the inferences of the advertisement may well be doubted without corroboration except that there is a brand of coffee on the market called 'A and B Coffee.'[3]

Garraghan says that most information comes from "indirect witnesses," people who were not present on the scene but heard of the events from someone else. He concedes that a historian may sometimes use hearsay evidence. He writes,

> In cases where he uses secondary witnesses, however, he does not rely upon them fully. On the contrary, he asks: (1) On whose primary testimony does the secondary witness base his statements? (2) Did the secondary witness accurately report the primary testimony as a whole? (3) If not, in what details did he accurately report the primary testimony? Satisfactory answers to the second and third questions may provide the historian with the whole or the gist of the primary testimony upon which the secondary witness may be his only means of knowledge. In such cases, the secondary source is the historian's 'original' source, in the sense of being the 'origin' of his knowledge. Insofar as this 'original' source is an accurate report of primary testimony, he tests its credibility as he would that of the primary testimony itself.[4]

The Unwitting Historian

Another caveat about using sources is that research in primary sources can often be an exercise in mental gymnastics. For example, should it appear that, during the English Civil Wars, a certain person was a Royalist – one who supported the monarchy as opposed to the Commonwealth – then an off-the-cuff statement in a will concerning an event that occurred in "the third year of the reign of good King Charles," might seem to confirm that idea since the writer was expressing the date in terms of the regnal calendar and the comment about "good King Charles" seems to settle any question about his political orientation. However, if the testator was documented as an officer of a Parliamentarian military brigade in opposition to the Crown as part of the Commonwealth forces, then the statements in the will might be a smoke screen, particularly if the will was written in the late 1650s. Further reading in the document might also demonstrate that the writer was quite shrewd: he might have realized that the Commonwealth was failing and the restoration of the monarchy was imminent. He perhaps included the statement as a sop to Royalists working within the Prerogative Court of Canterbury, where wills were probated and recorded word-for-word.[5]

Always look for "unwitting witnesses." A wealth of information might be gleaned; remember the "unwitting witnesses to history" who, in having made a comment on something they see as commonplace in their time, tell us about something that doesn't exist, or exists in a drastically altered form in our time.

Oral History

Grandma told us all kinds of stories, some of which just didn't sound right, but what if some of them were true?

Oral historians have recorded the reminiscences of survivors of the Nazi Holocaust, the Japanese-American internment on the U. S. West Coast and the Soviet gulags. Interviews have also captured the everyday experiences of families and communities, whether in inner cities, satellite suburbs or remote villages. When historians came to realize that women and racial and ethnic minorities were missing from the pages of most history texts, oral historians recorded their voices to construct a more diverse and accurate portrait of the past.

When oral histories are taken from third parties, the persons interviewed are due compensation for both their time and the use – and capture – of their memories. If their contribution to the historical record is included in a public television broadcast related to the subject on which they offered their recalling of those memories, they are due a royalty for the same reason that any performer should be compensated. That memory is their property; if they choose to share it, not only with the current public, but also with future historians through the archiving of their recorded interview, then they are due compensation for the same reason a photographer is due a royalty when one of his photographs is used by a publisher. Consequently,

"The Life & Times Of..."

taking an oral history can be an expensive and time-consuming effort, particularly if the recordings will be archived. The worth of the effort lies in the fact that oral history offers a first hand glimpse at the attitudes and emotions that history often fails to record, the chuckle at a memory brought to mind by an interviewer's question, or the sorrow that the person being interviewed only shares in the sound of their voice, with no details, or the everyday details that would be lost to history otherwise. Gottschalk described it thus:

> Most human affairs happen without leaving vestiges or a record of any kind behind them. The past, having happened, has perished with only occasional traces. To begin with, although the absolute number of historical writings is staggering, only a small part of what happened in the past was ever observed ... And only a part of what was observed in the past was remembered by those who observed it; only a part of what was remembered was recorded; and only a part of what was recorded has survived; only a part of what has survived has come to historians' attention; only a part of what has come to their attention is credible; only a part of what is creditable has been grasped; and only a part of what has been grasped can be expounded or narrated by the historian.[6]

Since the time and expenses related to archiving an oral history are great, then why do we, as historians go to that expense? If a future historian needs that information, why doesn't he go out and find his own person to interview? Cowan Shulman, in his book *Doing Oral History: a Practical Guide*, answered that question:

> When we conduct interviews, we are creating evidence. When the next historian comes along interested in another aspect or interpretation of the same topic, he or she should have access to the interviews we did. This is the very nature of history. Otherwise, I could hide all of my evidence to protect myself from competition and argument. Or I could make up anything I wanted and assert its truth citing interviews I supposedly conducted but would let no one else see. In other words, If we historians don't treat interviews seriously, we raise a series of problems that could hurt the profession as a whole.[7]

Oral history is often a practice unto itself. For those with an interest, Shulman's book is among the best beginning books in the field. The Oral History Association provides excellent guidance for further development of oral histories.

Oral Tradition

Oral tradition is different from oral history in that oral tradition is more concerned with the transmission of cultural values and lore than with specifics of history; it may contain historic elements but more often oral tradition is about maintaining cultural memory rather than historical memory. Even so, it has a place in historical investigation under certain criteria.

Oral tradition may be accepted as part of the historical record if it satisfies either two general conditions or all of six particular characteristics.

The general conditions are construed broadly; the first is that the tradition should be supported by an unbroken series of witnesses, reaching from the immediate and first reporter of the fact to the living mediate witness from whom we take it up, or to the one who was the first to commit it to writing

The second condition is that there should be several parallel and independent series of witnesses testifying to the fact in question.

The six particular characteristics are:

- The tradition must report a public event of importance, such as would necessarily be known directly to a great number of persons.
- The tradition must have been generally believed, at least for a definite period of time.
- During that definite period, it must have gone without protest, even from persons interested in denying it.

- The tradition must be one of relatively limited duration, of about 150 years, at least in cultures that excel in oral remembrance.
- The critical spirit must have been sufficiently developed while the tradition lasted, and the necessary means of critical investigation must have been at hand.
- Critical-minded persons who would surely have challenged the tradition — had they considered it false — must have made no such challenge.

Other methods of verifying oral tradition may exist, such as comparison with the evidence of archaeological remains.

Availability of Sources

Because the historian usually begins research from the perspective of someone who is faced with a giant jigsaw puzzle, with lots of missing pieces and without a picture of the finished product to guide the way, the historian gets to create the roadmap that guides the research.

As we take the slow walk from the cradle to the grave, we create literally thousands of documents. Thousands more are created about us. Thousands more may result if we go more than twenty-five miles from the place we were born, cross a national border, or from driving a car, owning a house or rental property, owning a business, getting married, having children, having municipal services, or any of a dozen activities.

Historical sources online are numerous; most are state archives or historical societies; many are university collections. Many county offices likewise have masses of data online. Including more than 5,000 archives available *online* at the state, province, and national level for English-speaking historians. A partial list is provided in Appendix 1. There are tens of thousands more, such as local libraries and local historical societies, all with information in some form. In any case, online sources must be subjected to, and withstand the same scrutiny as any other source; while there are good sources available on the Internet, there are also those that are tainted like any other might be.

As Douglas Adams said, "Don't Panic."[8]

Many of the resources concerning both people and place that local historians and family historians will use are concerned with are local – county and municipal offices and documents. A surprising number are available online and include:

- *Apprenticeship records*
- *Baptism or christening records*
- *Birth certificates*
- *Cemetery records and tombstones*
- *Census records*
- *Coroner's reports*
- *Death records*

- *Diaries, personal letters, family Bibles, scrapbooks and ephemera*
- *Directories - trade directories, street directories, telephone directories*
- *Earlier family histories*
- *Marriage certificates*
- *Military records*
- *Newspapers - both news items and advertisements*
- *Property records and contemporary maps*
- *Public records - social security records, Poor Law records (in Britain), registers of electors*
- *Tax records*
- *Wills and probate records*

Today many people are using these primary sources to recover their family history. But most of these records include only technical details of a person's life, such as their birth date, whom they married and so forth, but they contain very little about the person themselves such as their likes, dislikes, hobbies, hopes and dreams, occupation, memberships in guilds, societies or unions, and so forth. For modern researchers, family history websites and indexes are useful and they are often the main source of information. Some offer resources (e.g., census or civil registration records) that have previously only been available in microform or as hard copies; some are designed for individual researchers to share their information with others; some exist primarily to link people who share the same ancestors, or the same research interests. Indeed, many primary sources are available online. For those that are not, keep in mind that primary source material may be very old. If you are permitted to handle the material, you will be instructed by the archivist in the way to handle the material and should follow those instructions to the letter. These documents and goods are survivors from another time and should be treated with the utmost respect.

Private sources, such as Ancestry.com or the family and genealogical databases of the Church of Jesus Christ of Latter Day Saints can be invaluable; however, the family or local historian must remain acutely aware of the lack of verification and oversight in the privately submitted records.

Supposition, Research & Hypothesis

The historian must take documents, statements, oral histories, and traditional information into account, winnow it all down, and develop history from it. Determining which resources are appropriate to the project at hand uses the same agenda of questions, who, what, where, when, why, and how, to narrow down the choices. Having gathered and critically evaluated historical sources, the next step in preparing the history is determining which resources to use for the process, with a caveat:

- **Selective use** of sources in history may skew the investigation or prejudice it altogether. While we might be investigating the politics of a locale, it would be prejudicial to the investigation to *selectively use* only the sources from one political party that were damaging to the other political party. The result would not be history, but propaganda.

In this context, selective use means that historical sources are first chosen, and then information critical to their meaning and interpretation are omitted.

- **Selection of sources**, on the other hand, is necessary. For the local historian, the geographical limitation means a narrowing of scope that makes the *selection of sources* problematic only to the extent that the historian will need determine the applicability of the source's applicability to the specific research goals.

While selection of sources may mean not using sources that are outside the scope of an investigation or sources that duplicate each other, it also means going outside the bounds of the investigation as necessary, but only to the extent that it impacts the investigation or one of its elements.

Assessing each source in the proper historical context, the historian must harrow forgery, half-truth, deliberate distortion, the emotional high of patriotic propaganda, sly disinformation and, as previously noted, misinformation, to form and validate hypotheses by historical reasoning. Three methods are commonly used: Argument to the best

117

explanation, argument from analogy, and statistical inference.

The argument to the best explanation uses seven steps and begins with the formulation of a hypothesis. This hypothesis is a statement which is held to be true and which, when taken together with other statements about the subject, person, place, or event, implies other statements describing "present, observable data." This present, observable data may be artifacts, information found in documents, or physical features (buildings, landmarks) of the place.

For example, if it is generally believed that there was a blacksmith shop somewhere in the general area being studied, but the exact location of the former smithy is unknown, and the existence of a blacksmith shop in the general area is acknowledged in several documents (by tax receipts, comments in a newspaper contemporary to the smithy), then there is (1) a statement which is held to be true and (2) there are other present, observable data (the tax receipts and newspaper comments). The hypothesis would be that the blacksmith shop did indeed exist in the area, implying the presence of blacksmithing equipment, equine trade in the area and that there may have been a smith living nearby.

The second step is to determine whether the hypothesis that a blacksmith shop was in the area implies a greater explanatory scope than any other incompatible hypothesis about the same subject. If it's known that a smith lived in the area (his obituary appears in one of the contemporary newspapers), that the neighbourhood is on a street that was once a thoroughfare for horse drawn drayage (old city street information, trades information, railroad station lists) and that a large quantity of discarded horseshoes was once present (oral history from a person who remembers that a grandfather built a horseshoe pitch in the back yard of his home using old horseshoes found in the neighbourhood), and if that offers a greater explanatory scope (a greater variety of observation statements) than the fact that the 1902 World Horseshoe Pitching Contest was held in town, then we move to the third step.

In the third step we determine if the hypothesis is a better explanation than another. The hypothesis of a smithy in the area implies a smith, equipment, trade were present. The tax receipts (an observational statement) imply trade; the presence of the old (abandoned) horseshoes imply equipment, and the presence of the smith (the obituary) living in the area makes the presence of a smithy more likely than a horseshoe pitching contest.

The fourth step is one of plausibility: is the hypothesis more plausible than any other hypothesis about the same subject? In terms of the accepted truths about the area, is it more likely than not? The final test for plausibility is negative: if there are people who believe that a blacksmith shop was not present, are they greater in number than those who do? If evidence implies that a blacksmith shop was not present, is it more or less believable than the evidence that one was present?

All hypotheses are based, to a greater or lesser extend, on speculation and supposition. The fifth step has an element of negation and depends on how the hypothesis was arrived at: is the Hypothesis ("A") **based less on speculation and supposition about the past than other explanations implied by beliefs ("B") in the local area?** If hypothesis A has less speculative baggage than Hypothesis B, then Hypothesis A is <u>valid</u>.

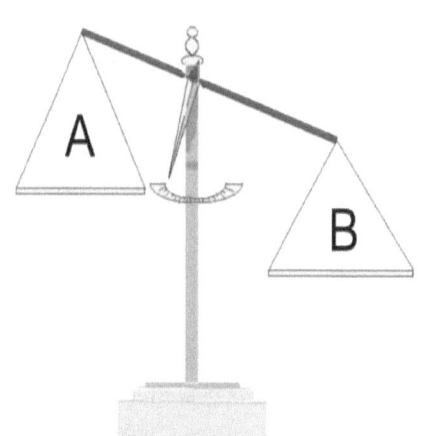

For a hypothesis to be true, it must imply fewer false observational statements than other explanations. If Grandma thought that Grandpa bought the horseshoes for his backyard pitch at the hardware store, but the uncles, aunts, brothers and sisters of the person who gave the oral history interview (see above) all said, when interviewed, that Grandma was wrong, then the process continues to the final step.

The hypothesis must "exceed other incompatible hypotheses about the same subject by so much, in characteristics 2 to 6, that there is little chance of an incompatible hypothesis, after further investigation, soon exceeding it in these respects." In other words, the hypothesis must be supported by a preponderance of the evidence.

In this case the existence by implication of the blacksmith shop is more widely recorded and reported than it would be if there were no blacksmith shop in the area (Test 2, above); and, although Grandma doesn't seem to believe that there was a blacksmith in the area, the uncles, aunts, brothers and sisters of the person interviewed were aware of by implication (Test 6, above). Therefore, since the scope and the strength of the explanation are so great that it explains the specific matter under investigation rather more thoroughly than any other explanation, it must be true.

If it walks like a duck and talks like a duck ….

Argument from Analogy

An argument from analogy, if sound, is either a "covert statistical syllogism" or better expressed as an argument to the best explanation. It is a statistical syllogism when it is "established by a sufficient number and variety of instances of the generalization"; otherwise, the argument may be invalid because properties 1 through n are unrelated to property n + 1, unless property n + 1 is the best explanation of properties 1 through n. Analogy, therefore, is uncontroversial only when used to suggest hypotheses, not as a conclusive argument.

Statistical Inference

The common example of statistical inference is stated

thusly:

Premise 1: There is probability of the degree p_1 that whatever is an A is a B.

Premise 2: It is probable to the degree p_2 that this is an A.

Therefore: Relative to these premises, it is probable to the degree $p_1 \times p_2$ that this is a B.

More simply put, this is a syllogism in probabilistic form, making use of a generalization formed by induction from numerous examples as a first premise

- In thousands of cases, the letters V.S.L.M. appearing at the end of a Latin inscription on a tombstone stand for *Votum Solvit Libens Merito*.
- From all appearances the letters V.S.L.M. are on this tombstone at the end of a Latin inscription.
- Therefore these letters on this tombstone stand for *Votum Solvit Libens Merito*.

One of the hazards of doing local history: you won't prove everything, no matter how hard you try.

Recording the Validated Hypotheses

When you arrive at each validated hypothesis by whichever means, it should be recorded, along with the means of validation and the information regarding the supporting documentation, including the name of the author, the date, place of origination, where the documentation or other source can be found at present, the reason for the existence of the source (why it was created), and how the source was located. It can be recorded on 3x5 index cards, a computer file or by any other means so long it is accessible. Several software packages are available for these note-taking tasks and are helpful if you are using a laptop computer in your research.

Interrogating & Interpreting Sources

When a historian interprets a document, what the historian is actually doing is making sense of it, both in terms of word (what's said) and the context (what's meant by the words, the style, even the document itself).

It's much like finding the meaning in an essay, a short story, or poetry. The historian takes raw information from the sources and makes it meaningful by relating it to our previous experiences, but with respect to the *proper historic context.*

We may, for example, respond to a loud noise by saying "That sounded like a car backfiring." When a person in an earlier century heard that loud noise, the response would more likely have been, "That sounded like a gunshot." In both cases, when we read or hear a sentence, we put the words together into a meaningful phrase, rather than just noting their separate meanings. Most everyday language is fairly straightforward and requires little interpretation. A liberal and a conservative who read a newspaper editorial decrying the death penalty may disagree with each other on that particular issue, but they will agree that the writer is against capital punishment: they won't have different interpretations of what the article means. Language, whether a document or oral history, usually requires special attention, however, when it is ambiguous or unclear. In order to clarify a sarcastic statement, for example, we may ask "What did the [writer, speaker, public servant] mean by that remark?" Because a historic source (including propaganda) presents us with more than one possible meaning, interpreting the information within the source requires care. Approaching sources critically helps maintain this complexity.

The interpretation of artifacts should most often be left to archaeologists. The horseshoes in the above example are artifacts. If they were in Grandpa's garage, they have lost their contextual value as archaeological artifacts, but remain historical artifacts nonetheless. The exception would be the mention of an artifact in a document or oral history since the document, not the object, is the historical source.

As always, a healthy skepticism should accompany this search for meaning just as it accompanied the search for the credibility and reliability of the source.

Generally, government documents are straightforward, with no hidden meanings. Even so, hidden messages of tragedy, joy, love, hate, disdain, fraternity – the whole range of human emotion – may be found in them and are often found in other documents. Family histories are often created as a memorial for the deceased, designed to preserve an individual's history for future generations. The readers will expect it to describe where the family originated from, name the members of the family and state who they married. Consequently, family histories, after having been subjected to the necessary interrogation to determine their quality as historical sources, can be invaluable to the local historian.

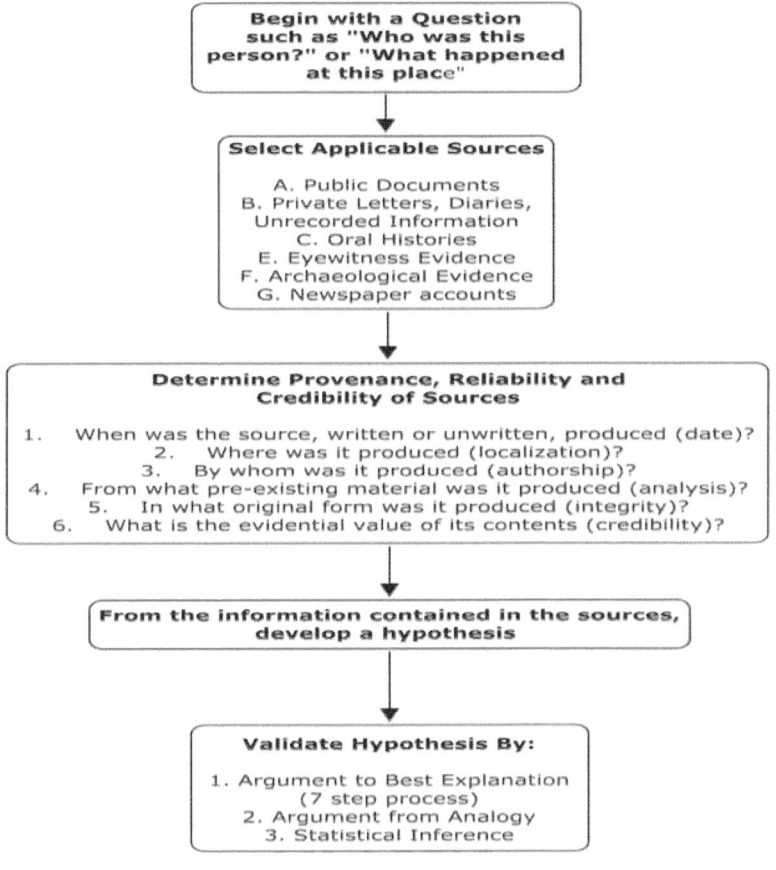

Figure 3.2 Validation of a Hypothesis

Citations

[1] Gilbert J. Garraghan, S. J., Jean Delanglez, Livia Appel, *A Guide to Historical Method* Fordham University Press, 1948

[2] Louis Gottschalk, *Understanding History: A Primer Of Historical Method,* New York, Alfred A. Knopf 1963

[3] *Understanding History*

[4] *A Guide to Historical Method*

[5] Will of Nicholas Badcocke, National Archives (UK), Catalogue Reference 11/250, Image Reference 1401

[6] *Understanding History*

[7] Donald A. Ritchie, *Doing Oral History: a Practical Guide,* Oxford University Press, 2003

[8] Douglas Adams, Stephen Moore, Simon Jones, Peter Jones, Roger Moore, *"Hitchhiker's Guide to the Galaxy,"* Music for Pleasure, 1981

"The Life & Times Of..."

Chapter 4

The Computer in Historical Research

The theory of probabilities is at bottom of nothing but common sense reduced to calculus. ~Laplace, Théorie analytique des probabilités, 1820

Personal computers are ubiquitous in today's world: we all have them, love them and hate them. They are the word processors at which we spend hours, writing scholarly works. They are the workstation where we will perform a vast amount of our work, from online research to preparing final copy. Fortunately, their capabilities extend far beyond that of a complicated typewriter. Historians use those extended capabilities of computers to make it easier to collect facts come from sources that include photos, maps, articles, books, public records, diaries and letters, web pages, interviews and personal observations, organize them and store them.

I. Doing History By The Numbers: Quantitative Analysis

Numbers are incredibly powerful. Even the phrase, "facts and figures," has a cachet of authority attached to it, simply because of the presence of the word, "figures." Numerical data, in the form of charts or tables can be used to visually describe the information presented in text either to clarify or to obscure.

Quantitative analysis, the use of statistics and statistical analysis techniques – rather than the use of mathematical material – is used in a social science such as history visually demonstrate matters discussed in text or to clarify or validate the research currently underway. Additionally, large data sets covering a range of experience have become recognized as a way of gaining a more representative and accurate picture of general experience and numerical analysis becomes essential. The computer, with its high-speed capabilities of storage, retrieval and comparison of masses of data has made quantitative analysis of data readily accessible to all.

Computers make it easy to retrieve facts that have been stored and to compare and sort facts to find patterns and to convert collections of sorted facts into prose and presentations that are clear, well organized and appropriate for the intended audience. Noted historian Robert Swierenga spoke to this capability in his monograph "Computers and Historical Research: a Personal Reflection"[1] as follows:

[Samuel] Hays put US census records and election statistics of the nineteenth century into computer files and discovered that ethnocultural groups had very distinct and predictable voting patterns at the local level. This so-called ethnocultural interpretation of American political history took the profession by storm in the 1970s. Since that time, quantitative methods in history have had difficulties, but the methodology has proved useful in ways not imagined at that time.

The personal computer's ability to store, retrieve, compare and process information for analysis by the local historian depends largely on two kinds of program. The first is the database, used primarily with non-numeric *qualitative* data and the other the spreadsheet, used primarily with numeric *quantitative* data.

Types of Data

Quantitative analysis can be used with some types of data and not others. The two main types of data are categorical data and numeric data, and each of those two types is divided into two additional sub-categories.

Nominal data are categorical; they are those data that we normally think of as words rather than data; a person's name, their type of employment, their religion, their worldview – all the things that aren't ordered or orderly about them.

Ordinal data are categorical as well. They are ordered and orderly, but without numbers. A household may be described as "middle class" without a specific yearly income level being given.

Numeric data – those written as numbers – include both interval data and ratio data. Interval data include those types where the interval is important: a table or graph describing rising global temperatures over a period of years uses two forms of interval data.

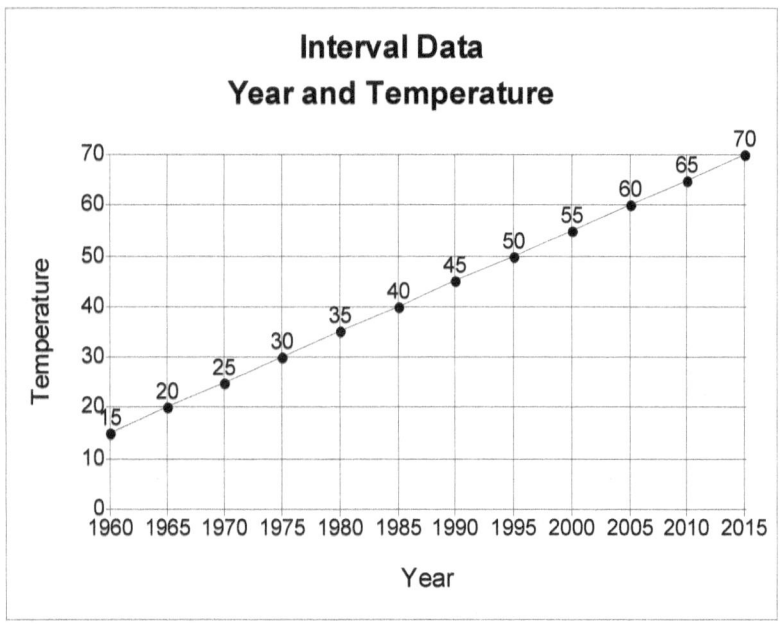

Figure 5.1 Interval Data. Data sets illustrative only

Ratio data is data where a comparison is made between two variables: A is forty times wealthier than B or C is six

The Computer in Historical Research

times older than D. The key to ratio data is that the units of measure must be common to each set of variables and must be able to be added, divided and averaged.

Intersection, Bourbon St. and…	Ratio of Bar Only vs Bar & Restaurant	Condition of Patrons
Conti	2	Somewhat
St. Louis	1	Slightly
Toulouse	3	Very
St. Peter	3	Extremely

Figure 5.2 Ratio of Bars to Bar/Restaurants at Intersections of Bourbon Street and the Level of Patron Sobriety at those locations. Source: Street Information, AAA Map of New Orleans.

These categories are not absolute. Nominal data arranged in a meaningful order become ordinal data and ordinal data may be taken as interval data depending on the method of display.

"There are three kinds of lies …"

Descriptive statistics are the most common and are usually represented in the form of an index, a histogram, a pie chart or a graph. In Chapter 2, the discussion of plagues and pestilences as a cause for population migration and immigration includes a pie chart, detailing the types of pandemics afflicting the European population between 1381 and 1831. That pie chart was developed from the

133

second chart, which detailed the locations and types of illnesses, by date.

Inferential statistics are those that can be used to infer a relationship such as cause and effect between two sets of data. The question, "Do crimes increase in frequency when unemployment rises?" might involve a comparison between unemployment statistics and crime statistics. In the case of inferential statistics, however, it must be noted that other factors might be involved. Comparisons between crime statistics and statistics involving other sociological or environmental factors in the specific locations under study would be necessary to rule out other factors which might have a greater or equal effect on the crime rates for that area.

Categorical Data		
Nominal (unordered)	Gives only qualitative information	Names, occupations, sex, religion, occupation
Ordinal (ordered)	Ranking or order is important	Social status, economic class
Numeric Data includes:		
Interval	Distance between values has meaning	Year, temperature
Ratio	Ratio of two values has meaning	Wealth, age, prices, wages

Figure 5.3 Data Types. Source: based on Hudson, *History by Numbers*, (OUP - NY 2000, p. 54, Table 3.1)

Undergoing Analysis

Time-series and *causal analysis* are probably the most familiar types of presentation, one that most people see several times a week, if not every day. These analyses are found in stock market reports. These reports are a time analysis, showing in numerical form the performance of various stocks over a period of days, weeks, months or years. For the local historian, this form of quantitative analysis might be used to compare sociological data drawn from a locale, such as income, mortality or educational levels over a period, allowing the historian to draw conclusions about the changing character and characteristics of the area under study. Time-series analysis allows the historian to observe how the change in one variable, such as wages in an area, is related to other variables in the same area over time.

The following is an example of a time-series analysis. The raw data presented in this example is used for illustrative purposes only, except that the hourly wage for 1939 is based on the *minimum wage* required by the Fair Labor Standards Act of 1939.

Raw Data: Wages for a laborer between 1900 and 1940

1900, $0.57/hr; 1905, $0.74/hr; 1910, $0.91/hr; 1915, $1.08/hr; 1920, $1.25/hr; 1925, $1.50/hr; 1930, unavailable; 1939, $0.25/hr.

Displaying the raw data as a graphic in tabular form as in

Figure 5.4 makes the above data the easier to comprehend: one picture is indeed worth a thousand words.

Year	Category of Employment	Wage/ Hr.	Significant Events
1900	Laborer	$0.05	
1905		$0.10	
1910		$0.15	
1915		$0.15	
1920		$0.23	
1925		$0.40	
1930	Data Unavailable		Worldwide Depression
1939		$0.25	Minimum Wage (FLSA)

Figure 5.4 - Tabular Format, Time-Series, Hourly Wages – Laborer. Data sets illustrative only.

The data can also be presented as a time-series graph as in Figure 5.5, below:

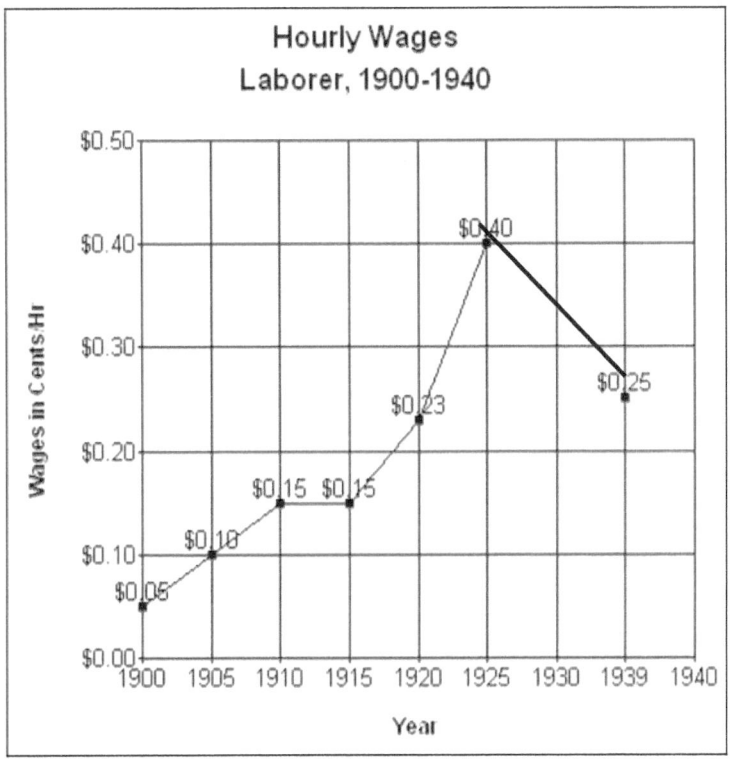

Figure 5.5 Time-Series graph, Hourly Wages – Laborer. Data sets illustrative only

These figures, both the line graph and the table, are graphic representations of descriptive statistics.

Both of the following figures are tabular presentations, but of two different sets of raw data. One is a time-series presentation of the price of one pound of bread between 1900 and 1939. The second is shows both the price of the bread, the hourly wages of a laborer for the same period and the number of hours, or part of an hour, that the laborer must work to earn that pound of bread.

Raw Data: Price of One Pound of Bread between 1900 and 1939: 1900, $0.05; 1905, $0.10; 1910, $0.15; 1915, $0.15; 1920, $0.23; 1925, $0.40; 1930, No Data Available; 1939, $0.05

Tabular Presentation:

Year	Price of 1 lb. of Bread
1900	$0.05
1905	$0.10
1910	$0.15
1915	$0.15
1920	$0.23
1925	$0.40
1930	Data Unavailable
1939	$0.05

Figure 5.6 Time-Series, Cost of Bread. Data Sets for illustrative purposes only

Figure 5.4 combines the descriptive statistical data derived from Figure 5.1 and Figure 5.3, yielding the information contained in the last column representing what part of an hour the laborer must work to earn enough money to buy one pound of bread. From this, we may be able to infer other data, including the fact that, following a major depression, the price of goods will (eventually) drop and, if government introduces wage supports, the purchasing power of the consumer may benefit.

Year	Price of 1 lb. of Bread	Hourly Wage, Laborer	Hours Worked for 1 lb Of Bread
1900	$0.05	$0.05	1.00
1905	$0.07	$0.10	0.70
1910	$0.09	$0.15	0.60
1915	$0.12	$0.15	0.80
1920	$0.18	$0.23	0.78
1925	$0.35	$0.40	0.87
1930		Data Unavailable	
1939	$0.05	$0.25	0.20

Figure 5.7 Hours Worked For 1 lb. of Bread. Data sets for illustrative purposes only.

Because of the proliferation of the personal computer, *large-scale studies* such as those involving demographic data and those where massive amounts of data are examined and analyzed are more practical for a historian to undertake. However, the geographic limitation inherent in local history will significantly decrease the scale of "large scale."

The Elements of Display

Data set: A data set is a group of data selected or gathered to help answer a particular question, usually made up of a series of cases (see below).

Case: One or more pieces of information related to a

"The Life & Times Of..."

particular unit of investigation. In a list of families on a street with names, addresses and telephone numbers – the information often found in a city directory – each family on the list ("Jones, Michael" in the example below) would be a case.

Jones, David	743 Sheridan Dr	766-2193
Jones, Michael	**1762 Hassell St**	**723-4937**
Jones, Patrick	9 Otranto Way	544-1729
Jones, Stephen	739 Norfolk Dr	795-3612
Jones, Thomas	50 Gibbes St	722-1549

Figure 5.8 Illustration of Case. Data sets illustrative only.

Variable: Each piece of information related to a case is a variable. In the list of families mentioned above, the name is a variable, the address is a variable and the telephone number is a variable.

Jones, Michael	=	Variable
1762 Hassell St	=	Variable
723-4937	=	Variable

Figure 5.9 Illustration of Variable. Data sets illustrative only.

Three terms describe the format in which data is displayed:

Data matrix: A way of organizing and tabulating a data set. Each case has a row to itself and each variable has a column, as in a spreadsheet.

Vector or **Field:** A column (or row) of information in a data matrix.

Cell: A single unit of information (the name *or* the address *or* the phone number in the above example.)

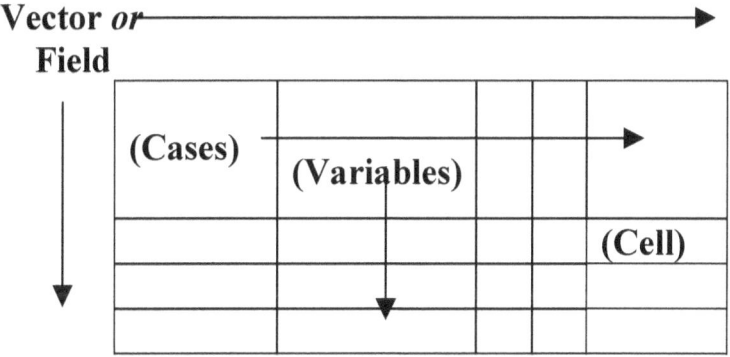

Fig. 5.10 The data matrix and components

Standard Methods of Presenting Tables & Figures: The Rules

Although there are numerous forms of chart and graph, there are conventions regarding the labelling and placement of information, including column and row headers, placement of vectors of data, titling, and sourcing.

Table and figures must:

1. Have a title which briefly describes content, time period covered and units of measurement used
2. Give details of the precise source of the information they contain.

Columns and row headings should be brief and self-explanatory, with units of measurement clearly indicated.

Vectors of data which are to be compared should be close together and derived statistics such as percentages and averages should be next to the figures in which they relate, either in brackets or within the same cell or in an adjacent vector.

Which Chart For What Purpose?

The manner in which data are presented can be almost as important as the data itself simply because, as the old truism goes, one picture is worth a thousand words. If the type of presentation does not present the data in an easily understandable form, the information the data represent becomes useless or, worse, confusing. The most common presentation forms are:

1. The *Bar Chart*, used for nominal, ordinal or interval data, it better presents the information collected in frequency distributions.
2. The *Histogram* resembles a three-dimensional bar chart, with the width of the bars proportional to the

class interval and an area proportional to the frequency.
3. The *Pie Chart* is the easiest, clearest way to present the proportions of the discrete elements that constitute a whole.
4. *Line Graphs* are best for time-series or other interval data.

Interrogating Data

Like any other historical source, the provenance and credibility of data must be evaluated by the historical method and judged by the historian's critical thinking. In addition, there are questions specific to the data set itself. How were the data collected? Was the manner of collection consistent with good historical practice? How was the data collected and what errors might the data set contain? Why were the data collected?

Many of the same problems which are inherent with the collection and archiving of oral history may appear: are the data prejudiced because of the collector's prejudices and are they slanted to meet the collector's needs? Data may be partial or incomplete, since they may be the only surviving documentation rather than a truly representative data set.

The final question to be asked, assuming the data set survives the above interrogatories successfully, is, "Does this data meet the needs of the current study without prejudicing the history unnecessarily?"

Grouping Data: Frequency Distribution

Frequency distribution is a description of how often an item of information – a variable – occurs within a data matrix. It is one of the most useful tools used to call certain types of data to the attention of the reader, particularly those data obtained from certain types of sources, particularly those such as:

- Genealogical studies
- Data on birth and mortality rates from vital statistics offices and church records
- Data on educational achievements
- Tax records
- Analysis of the age of individuals within each group at various milestones in the individual's life.
- Information on family makeup
- Prosopography, which is more fully explained below.
- Quantifiable geographic data such as elevations and soil types

For example, if a given name or family name seems to appear often either within a neighborhood or a family tree, determining the frequency distribution might yield clues that the local or family historian would find useful.

Distribution is defined as the full range of values for any one variable, that is, all of the values in one column vector as show in Figure 5.11 below. In that figure, it gives the surnames of men, then in two columns, their given names are displayed. The Distribution in each column of given names would simply be a list of the names in that column, with no regard to the surnames, nor with regard to the given names listed in any other column.

Surname	Given Name Column 1	Given Name Column 2
Jones	Patrick	Michael
Smith	David	Patrick
Watson	David	John
Holmes	Sherlock	Myron

Figure 5.11 Data Matrix of Imaginary Names

A table showing the distribution of a variable would appear as if the historian had simply duplicating the all of the variables in a single column, putting that information into a tabular form.

The distribution in Column 1 (Given Names) is shown in Figure 5.12.

Given Names
Patrick
David
David
Sherlock

Figure 5.12. Distribution of Given Names in Column 1 of Figure 5.11.

"The Life & Times Of…"

Frequency is the *number of times* any one value of a variable occurs: how many times does each given name in Column 1 occur?

Given Names	Frequency
David	2
Patrick	2
Michael	1
John	1
Myron	1
Sherlock	1
Total	8

Figure 5.13 Frequency of Given Names in Column 1

Frequency Distribution is a tabulation that shows the frequency with which selected variables appear within the data set.

Alphabetic Group, Initial Letter of Given Name	Frequency in Group	Percentage of Population
K - O	3	37.5%
O - Z	3	37.5%
A - J	2	25%
Total	8	100%

Figure 5.14. Frequency distribution of imaginary given names

Figure 5.14 shows that the frequency distribution of given

names throughout the chosen segments of the alphabet.

Frequency distribution and Local History

Was the place being studied a "tough" area? Did the families within the area produce a higher-than-average number of criminals? An inspection of local jail records, when subjected to an analysis of the frequency distribution of the incarcerated offender's addresses, may provide this information. An inspection of tax records and an analysis of the frequency distribution of delinquency may suggest that the population of a place was undergoing financial difficulties or it may indicate that the people in the area were either better able to cope with a particular widespread financial downturn or otherwise unaffected by the historical downtown.

Age at Death	Frequency of Death	Deaths as a Percentage of Population
0-9	42	3%
10-19	24	1.7%
19-45	200	14.3%
Total	266	19%

Figure 5.15. Frequency Distribution of Deaths resulting from 1917 Flu Epidemic, as a percentage of neighborhood population of 1,400. Data set is illustrative only.

An analysis of the frequency distribution of vital records within a place can be used to determine if birth and mortality rates within a place were excessive. As an example, the 1917 influenza epidemic may have had a higher or lower incidence of mortality among certain age groups within a neighborhood, when compared to similar neighborhoods within an area. The frequency distribution for deaths due to influenza, together with a percentage of the total population of the neighborhood is illustrated in Figure 5.15, with an imaginary population of 1400.

There are two additional conventions for presenting frequency distribution data. The first is that frequency distributions should always have a total figure (see Figure 5.15 above). The second is to insure that grouped distributions must not have any overlap between categories or class intervals.

Measuring the Average

Baseball great Satchel Paige said, "Ain't no man can avoid being born average, but there ain't no man got to be *common*."

The mean, median and mode are three types of average. The *mean*, also called the arithmetic mean, is a simple average. This might be the sum of all variables in a single field, divided by the number of variables in the field:

$$\frac{13.0+9.5+6.5+6+5.5}{5} = 8.1$$

Figure 5.15 Determining the Mean Value (in thousands of dollars) of housing in Imaginary Neighborhood A

The mean is an average, but it may not show the whole picture. If the mean value of a house in a neighborhood is $6,500 in 1880, then the historian might compare the mean value of housing in one neighborhood against the mean value of housing for that same year in another neighborhood and gain some rough insight as to the desirability of the housing within one location as opposed to another.

However, what if the mean value is the same in two neighborhoods, and one is described in historical sources as well kept and the other as run down except for one house? The *median* value of the housing in the two areas might offer some clarification.

The **median** is the measurement at the midpoint of a list:

Median Value, Neighborhood A	Median Value, Neighborhood B
$13,000	$19,500
$9,500	$9,000
$6,500	**$4,500**
$6,000	$3,500
$5,500	$3,000
Mean: $8,100	Mean: $8,100

Figure 5.16 The median in this example is $6,500

While the mean values for both Neighborhood *A* and Neighborhood *B* are equal, the median values are not, meaning that there were more houses valued at less than $6,500 in Neighborhood *B* than in Neighborhood *A*. The median, therefore, may be viewed as a watershed, a divide by which the frequency distribution within a group may be judged.

The *mode* or *modal distribution* is the variable that occurs most frequently in a frequency distribution:

Housing Unit Value	Housing Units valued at this level	Percentage of Houses
$5,500 – $6,500	**311**	72%
$6,501 – $9,500	20	22%
$9,500 - $13,500	12	6%
Total	430	100%

Figure 5.17 Frequency Distribution of Housing Values in fictional Neighborhood A. The mode in this example is 311.

Housing Unit Value	Housing Units valued at this level	Percentage of Houses
$3,000 - $3,500	**311**	72%
$3,501 – 9,000	20	22%
$9,500 – $19,500	12	6%
Total	430	100%

Figure 5.18 Frequency Distribution of Housing Values in fictional Neighborhood B. The mode in this example is 311.

Figures 5.17 and 5.18 show that while the most expensive

housing units are in Neighborhood B, 72% of the housing units in Neighborhood A, are valued at $6,500 or more whereas in Neighborhood B, 72% of the housing units are valued at $3,500 or less.

While the above examples seem to be aimed at the local historian, these same principles can be used by the family historian to analyze family records as well: births, deaths and causes of death, religious preferences – the list is only limited by the imagination. Still, these are only averages. How can we determine how variations – the statistical black sheep called *dispersions* – are distributed around these averages?

Variance and Standard Deviation

The mean is one way to express distribution (of wealth, of age, of home values) in a one-size-fits-all manner. If the mean is the straight line that lies between all the variables from which it is made up, then *variance* is a way to express how far the variables are spread out (dispersed) from the mean.

Standard deviation is one more way that the dispersion of variables around the mean: it's the square root of the variance. Nearly all spreadsheet programs have an automated statistical function for variance and standard deviation.

Prosopography

Prosopography has been defined as an independent science

of social history embracing genealogy, onomastics (the study of proper names of all kinds and the origins of names.) and demography. Prosopography is an investigation of the common characteristics of an historical group, whose individual biographies may be largely untraceable, by means of a collective study of their lives. Prosopographical research has the aim of learning about patterns of relationships and activities through the study of collective biography, and proceeds by collecting and analyzing statistically relevant quantities of biographical data about a well-defined group of individuals. It will be of interest to the local historian who is, for example, undertaking a statistical analysis of family groupings within a given locale. It may also be of great interest to family historians when dealing with Native American ancestors, where information can be less than complete. Database systems are an ideal tool for this purpose, since records kept by the Bureau of Indian Affairs are sketchy; the application of propographical principles may demonstrate kinship or other relationships where a simple list of names might not.

Basic training in and some interesting information on the subject, as well as the *Prosopography of Anglo Saxon England*, is available online through Linacre College at the University of Oxford.

It is not the aim of this text to produce a finished statistician nor, probably, is it the aim of the local historian to become a finished statistician. A very good text for the historian who wants to become a more accomplished quantitative historian is *History By Numbers*, written by Pat Hudson of Cardiff University.

GIS Systems

Another computer-based system very useful to the historian is GIS. Geographic Information Systems (GIS) are computer-based systems for the capture, storage, analysis and management of data based on location. They allow users to relate multiple layers of information in a geographic framework. GIS is becoming increasingly important in historical studies, for example to study changes in population density, following the shifting population over a period of time defined by the user.

One of the most often cited pitfalls of GIS in history is that their use requires some specialized training; however, they are readily available in a simplified form through some web-based services like Google Earth, which allows the user to customize the map/image in most of the ways that a PC-based GIS system does. While some outside training may be necessary to fully use such limited systems, they nonetheless provide some level of serviceability with only minimal assistance.

Uses of GIS might include tracking or displaying historic employment patterns, industrialization, famine, pandemics, income, population shifts or any other human condition or field of endeavour that may be digitized, either numeric or non-numeric.

Aerial photography or Geographic Information Systems may also provide clues to the past, showing changes in terrain in an easily interpreted manner. GIS is being used increasingly in the mapping of some Civil War battlefields, with some surprising results.

Extensive training in the use of commercial GIS systems is readily available online and many colleges and universities offer varying levels of training in GIS. Some of these courses might be of service to the local historian. The potential for using GIS applications in local history is largely untapped. As yet, the potential uses in family history seem to have been unexplored.

One caveat on using maps and GIS systems: never, ever forget to "walk the ground" in the area under study. Some things can never be duplicated by photographs or maps and historical clues, such as the relationship between a rise in the terrain and the location of a stand of two-century-old trees can only be seen on the ground, and that relationship – perhaps the sight lines along which shots were fired in a Revolutionary skirmish – may have had an effect on the history of a place.

The computer is a useful tool for history, but the historian must remember that the writing of history, whether local or family, depends on the sources and types of sources available, and on the judgement of the historian as to what information is important to the project at hand.

Citations

[1] **Robert P. Swierenga**, "Computers and Historical Research: Personal Reflections" A paper delivered at Spring Arbor College, September 24, 1999, to the Regional History Meeting

Pat Hudson, *History by Numbers*, Oxford University Press, 2000

"The Life & Times Of..."

Chapter 5

Synthesis: Turning Research Into History

The past is malleable and flexible, changing as our recollection interprets and re-explains what has happened.
~Peter Berger

Turning a mosaic of hypotheses into a cohesive historical picture is a tricky business at best and often a source of controversy within the discipline of history. Writing history can be as simple as writing a comprehensive obituary, or as complex as writing a novel. In either case, the historian must be sensitive to the facts presented in the historical resources and the truth revealed by those sources, whether directly or indirectly.

Where the local historian researches an area and its occupants and the records lead to a conclusion that seems to make sense, the family historian researches a relative and finds information that suggests why that relative did the things that led to the creation of a historical record.

"The Life & Times Of..."

For both the local and family historian, the process is the same and begins with the development of a hypothesis, a *potential* explanation of what happened or why. Often, multiple hypotheses can be formulated from the same data. If a hypothesis that makes sense when tested against the parameters established for the study and is deemed correct, it's successful. The problem with this is that an accumulation of apparently successful hypotheses, whether in local history or family history, tends to be viewed as circumstantial evidence of truth; the cumulative idea becomes popular in the community, whether the community is that of distinct individuals, as in local history, or the community found within a family. The problem with the success of circumstantial evidence is that a hypothesis can be so strongly supported that it becomes history, even though it's fundamentally *wrong*. The decision of the historian to accept or reject an accumulation of hypotheses is the fundamental challenge facing every historian.

The historian has three choices to make about the inclusion of a successful hypothesis: reject the hypothesis as potentially true but wrong; remain uncommitted about the hypothesis ("let's see where the history leads us") or accept the hypothesis as truth. There are no guarantees that what the historian chooses to include in the final version of the history will accurately reflect the actual history. In choosing any one of the three, the historian makes his case and the work continues. This means that when the historian makes a choice, the hypothesis chosen is transformed from a simple hypothesis into an element of history.

While there may not always be objective criteria by which to determine which hypotheses are correct or to help decide which should be consigned to the written history or the scrap heap, the criteria established at the beginning of the study serve as the historian's guideposts. Consequently, writing history is not an exact science. Historians are inquisitive people by nature. They want to know why a document was produced, who created it and what they were trying to say. They want to have as much evidence to rummage through as is humanly possible and, when they have finished their rummaging, they will produce a learned work telling the world the story of the love, joy, hate, despair or human stupidity that the document (or artifact) actually represents.

Sometimes, however, when direct information is missing but the situation is obvious, they will resort to using "the historical imagination" to fill in gaps when the documentation suggests, but does not specify known fact. The challenge of records lost in courthouse fires, hard-copy records misfiled or electronic records that seem to have dropped off the face of the earth may mean that while the historian can follow the subject from point A to point C, and there is no sure and certain knowledge of what happened between A and B or if there ever was a B.

The Historical Imagination

There will always be missing records, there will always be

"*The Life & Times Of...*"

conflicting testimony, and there will always be points of view contrary to the one which seems the most likely to be correct. In its most common form, history can be as simple as a recitation of the tested hypotheses, or as elaborate as a novel. Building a cohesive picture of the past will depend on the ability of the historian to establish the place of the proven hypotheses and describe their importance and effects despite these apparently insurmountable gaps in the record.

Historian Robin George Collingwood was born in the late 19th century and worked as a philosopher and historian between 1910 and 1943. Collingwood saw a fundamental difference between history and the natural sciences in that the scientific method of observing, measuring, classifying, and generating of physical laws was—while a perfectly legitimate way of "knowing" the natural world—insufficient for history. However, as Collingwood pointed out, history is fundamentally different because historical events, regardless of size, have both an observable objective element, and a subjective element "described in terms of thought." The objective element was the part of the historical event that could have been touched or seen, like a document or artifact. The subjective element consists of the thoughts and emotions of the people involved in the event before, during, and after the fact. Collingwood also stated that historical knowledge is fundamentally different from knowledge about the natural world in that it involves both the observable and the unobservable.

While "imagining" might be seen as a flight of fancy,

Collingwood saw it otherwise and, to demonstrate his point, he provided the following example:

> "If I imagine the friend who lately left my house now entering his own, the fact that I imagine this event gives me no reason to believe it unreal."

Historical Imagination is nothing more than a process to re-construct the past, pictures, ideas or concepts in our minds and thus the process should not be equated with either a flight of fancy *or* the truth. It reconstructs pictures, ideas and concepts that are related to what really happened and what was really thought, whereas a literary work comes solely from what Lynn Speer Lemisko calls the "fanciful" imagination:

> While he noted that both use imagination to construct a narrative that has continuity and coherence, the novelist's entire construction or picture can be derived out of "fanciful" imagination. The historian's construction, on the other hand, is constrained by two important elements that can be ignored by a novelist. The historian's picture must be localized in a space and time that has actually existed and it must be related to the evidence that the historian gathers from sources. If the historian cannot demonstrate any link between the picture that she/he constructs and this evidence, then it will be assumed that the picture is merely fantasy. The key difference, then,

is that historians must use sources as evidence in their imaginative process. [1]

While a flight of fancy isn't appropriate as historical imagination, a shrewd guess based on some part of the evidence, is. These shrewd guesses must be based on some element found within the evidence; they must be subjected to the same scrutiny as any other part of the evidence using the argument to best explanation, argument from analogy and statistical inference. As a practical matter, if the shrewd guess is within the historical context and supported by the evidence, and no other explanation is forthcoming, the shrewd guess will stand as a valid hypothesis. The hypothesis is then evaluated against the criteria for validity, credibility, reliability, and authority.

The opening sentence of this book, "American history is based on a true story," is accurate. The tales we tell ourselves, the changes in the manner of presentation, the idea of a single event viewed from many perspectives, all influence history both as a record and a concept. Most family and local historians will be concerned with writing history as it was, a concept of long standing known as "historical empiricism." in which the historian neither judges the past nor makes predictions of future; rather, the historian depicts – recreates – the past. This means that the historical context – how the matter was perceived by the person living then becomes even more important. This historical context will include the external influences upon that person and the larger effects of elements of other historical processes, for example, the discovery of gold in

California in 1848 and the influx of European settlers trying to get away from the near-revolutions and minor wars occurring that year, as well as the more mundane aspects of life in that foreign country we call "the past."

Meaning & Theories of Meaning: Interpreting Sources

Interpreting history is also an exercise in both historical awareness and historical context. When a historian interprets a document, what the historian is actually doing is making sense of it, both in terms of the words – what's said – and context – what's *meant* by the words, the style, even the document itself. It is much like finding the meaning in an essay, a short story or poetry; the source may express its meaning in veiled hints or in plain thoughts whose context is unfamiliar to us. The source may be a letter, a public document, even an element not readily noticeable but full of meaning, as in a film company's opening broadside during a specific time.

In the early 1940s, RKO Studio changed the opening advertising sequence for all of their movies. Their movies completed prior to that time opened with a picture of a spinning globe, atop which was a radio transmitter's antenna tower, and an audio overlay of a radiotelegrapher tapping out Morse code: as each letter in code was completed, a letter appeared on the screen, finally spelling out the phrase, "An RKO Radio Picture."

With "War Fever" gripping America and the Lend-Lease

program to the Great Britain in full swing, the opening sequence was changed ever so slightly to include the code letter "V" (dot-dot-dot, dash), followed by a slight pause, at the beginning and end of the code spelling out the company's name. The letter "V" never appeared on screen, but the dot, dot, dot, dash sequence was popular at the time as shorthand for a slogan which became a wartime mantra, "V for Victory!"[1] In movies completed after World War II, the "V," with its patriotic overtones was dropped and the opening reverted to its original "code transmission."

It is the place of the historian to find the meaning behind such veiled hints, and place that meaning in the proper historical context. In the above example, the context might have been the outrage and moral indignation the theater-going public felt over the Japanese attack on Pearl Harbor, or simply a show of support for the soldiers, sailors and Marines fighting in the War. The reason for the change in the opening sequence may have been a genuine show of patriotism, or an appeal to the patriotic feelings of the moviegoers. It might have allowed the moviegoer a personal identification with the "V for Victory!" slogan and sentiment. At that point, interpretation begins, as the historian seeks the meaning of the event. A healthy skepticism should accompany this search for meaning just as it accompanied the search for the credibility and reliability of the source.

An interpretive investigation might determine, for example, that a deed for a family home, signed by a county public official, like a county sheriff – as the seller – in Oklahoma in 1929 may not, in the proper historical context, be the devastating family tragedy one might imagine:

- **What** is the subject of the document? The **house**, which was sold.
- **Who signed the deed?** The sheriff. Was the sale made under duress? Was the house seized because of a non-payment of the mortgage? Or had the home simply been transferred to the sheriff for sale?
- **Where** was the home? The property was located in Oklahoma.
- Was the property **urban or rural**?
- **When** was property sold? 1929.
- **When** in 1929?

Unless interpreted fully, completely and properly, from a hypothesis based on information from pertinent sources that were reliable and credible by an objective standard, and in the proper historical context, the incomplete answer to the question, "why was the home sold?" might skew a family or local history considerably.

From the facts, it appears that the sheriff sold the property. Does the document mention why? If sold under duress, as in a sale for back taxes or following the seizure by a mortgage holder, the *banker* would be the seller, not the sheriff.

Looking to the historical context, the Great Depression

165

officially began with the stock market crash of October 29, 1929, that heralded the onset of the Depression. If the home was sold before that date, the sale probably was *not* related to market and business failures during that time.

The property was located in Oklahoma. If it was a farming property, the sale didn't occur during the time of the "Oklahoma Dust Bowl," which resulted from agrarian failures before 1929 and didn't become a reality until the 1930s.

If the property was sold before the Great Depression, without going to the bank in foreclosure, the "why?" question loses some of its urgency; further research might reveal that the house was sold to the sheriff, who did not file his purchase deed until he sold the property to another party.

If no other evidence exists, the questions remain unanswered. Five-sixths of the year 1929 was not hounded by financial disaster and the other circumstances indicate that the sale was not forced by foreclosure. The historian, having successfully interrogated and interpreted the evidence, knows only that the home was sold and, with regard to its sale, should report only that much, subject to the use of the historical imagination.

Another example of this interrogation of a source might be asking who was the first settler in an area and what the area was like at that time. What were (or are) its geological characteristics, such as terrain, climate and soil? Where were its resources of water, what game was present? Why was this area chosen and how did the area develop from a frontier – remember, in the historical context of 1607, the frontier was less than a hundred meters from the edge of the Atlantic – into a community? How did physical features such as cliffs and ridges effect that development? How did the settlers change the face of the landscape over time and how did those changes affect the community under study? As a practical matter, county recorder or deed offices will have maps (or copies on microfiche) of old maps, perhaps going back to the first surveys of the area. Comparison of these maps to the ongoing development of the area will provide insight into the pace and direction of that development.

History as a Team Effort

From time to time, it will be necessary for the historian to seek outside help in fields as diverse as naval architecture, agriculture, law, gambling, business, weaving, shoemaking, the arts, geophysics and various religions in the course of research. Further, neither local history nor family history is a solitary practice – the lone researcher huddled in the archive for a great length of time is probably dead, mummified, and covered with cobwebs.

As work progresses, that it will also be advantageous to have external support in the form of other local historians, perhaps a friendly geologist or expert in construction. Most important, though, will be other local historians who have encountered the same problems with sources and solved them. Local historical societies are priceless sources of information, local legend and physical artifacts.

Writing the History

The final step in the project is actually writing the history, using all the note cards, photocopies and other paraphernalia associated with the effort.

Distilling those notes into a cohesive history should be undertaken in a logical manner, following the classic "who, what, where, when, why?" order:

Writing local history is not easy. It means many trips to out of the way places, crawling through old documents – either in hand or on microfiches – searching for the one piece of information that gives insight into your research, and doing this day after day. Or spending hours listening to tapes that record the ramblings of people best described as old curmudgeons as they describe everything but what you needed for your research. Your reward might be that, as you dig through the mountains of information available, you discover some long lost corner of history that no one has fully researched. Even if the general matter has been done to death, no one has truly researched this particular information adequately, and you find some nugget that casts the previously done histories into doubt and disarray.

There are only six questions in local history: who, what, where, when, why and how. Writing history begins with curiosity about the answers these questions. If you ask

Turning Research Into History

these questions, both *of* documentation and people and *about* documentation and people, you'll be deluged with more information than you can handle. You then face the task of sorting through the information to determine what will answer your initial question and, from this mass of data, forming opinions which, when tested against either the available data or (using your historical imagination) that information which fits without any fudging, will become viable hypotheses, to be interpreted as history.

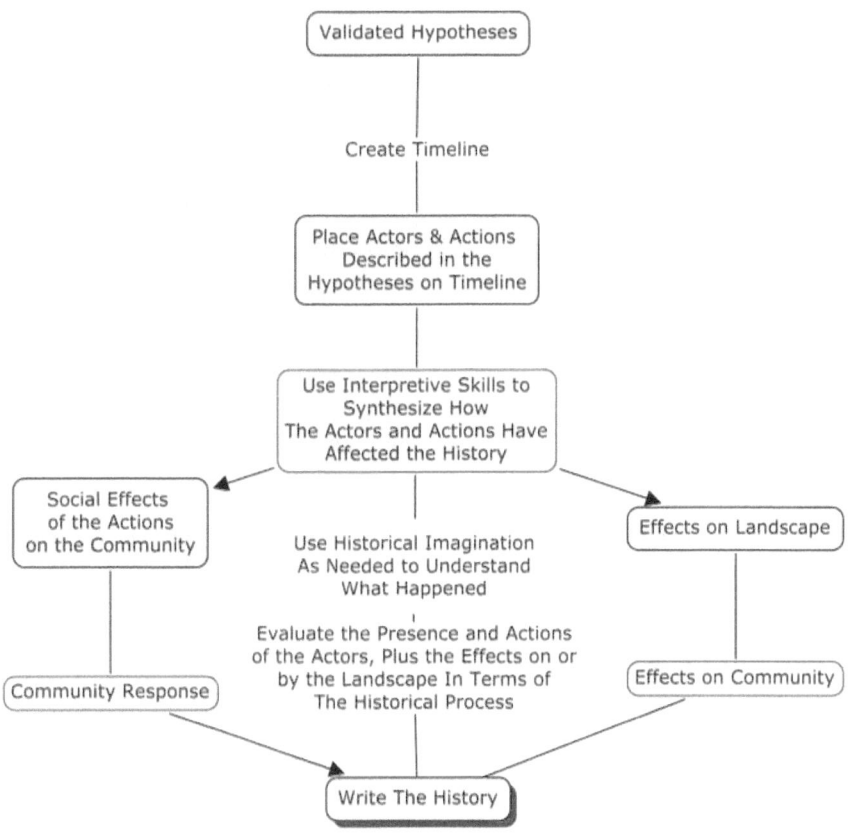

History as Literature?

What's left to do, but to go out and write the history? Remember though, to do it well. The history written today will carry our own prejudices and personality forward to future historians, who will be questioning our work as a historical source. They will have the advantage of hindsight, which is supposedly 20/20, as is ours, and they may find our work quaint or worse. Even so, we must contribute our share, since to do otherwise would be worse than doing nothing. Imagine a discussion of the 20th Century, which lacks the effects on local history of both the 1960s and the Vietnam War, half-a-world away and you can understand the need for a workmanlike effort.

Even so, history doesn't have to be dull. If it's dull, no one will want to read it, even if they like history.

Up to this point, no mention has been made of historical theory, since most historical theories seem intended to cloud the view of the local or family historian. However, one particular theory of history defines historical work as "a verbal structure in the form of a narrative prose discourse that classifies past structures and processes in order to explain what they were by representing them as models."[2] In other words, we tell a story based on a series of things that have happened in the past.

This theory asserts that the historian "makes" history by asking the questions who, what, why, where, when and how, by deciding which events to include or exclude, by arranging events in a certain order and by stressing some events while wholly ignoring others.

Another point this theory makes is that, every history written will have at its core a plot – obviously, the reason why the history is being written finds its basis in the first twitches of curiosity about the subject. Will the history be a comedy? A tragedy? A satire? Or even a romance?

Whether you agree with this appraisal of historiography (the writing of history) or not, if historians provide no more than "just the facts," the historian still has the ability to determine to interrogate one source and not another; and we must form our historical opinions on the information we have discovered, and present them.

Organizing the Presentation

The two most common forms for presenting history are the narrative, where a narrator "recreates" the history, and the other is the descriptive, where the historian describes the events, persons, places and events through the presentation of the documentation and the evidence.

For the local historian, character and setting become "people" and "place." Conflict might be represented by the people within a geographically delimited area demanding a certain concession from the government (the right to sell liquor on Sunday in some states, for example) and resolution by the final settlement of the question. Does a champion for one side of the conflict arise in the

171

neighborhood? Do the neighbors shun the Champion? What does the Champion do? Hopefully, a choice between the narrative and the descriptive will mean that even the most boring local history seems to be written in a way that is both history and readable.

In either case, the suggested method of organizing the presentation is as follows:

1. Develop a general timeline from the notes, for example, "from 1854 to 1890" or by the specific dates covered by the notes, "from January 15th, 1854 to December 17th, 1903."
2. Determine who the actors were at specific points on that timeline, and what evidence is associated with each point on the timeline – not just the occurrence itself, but the evidence of its ongoing effects as well.
3. Determine how the actions of the persons involved at each specific point affected the physical locale, or how those actions were effected by the locale: were there earthworks on the property? Or were earthworks (the remains of a Civil War fortification) removed from the property?
4. Determine the effects, if any, of the actors on the community and the effect of changes to the locale on the community or, if the community as a whole made changes on the locale, how did these changes affect the community?

5. Use the historical imagination as necessary, within the historical context.
6. Remember the historical process. Look for the process at work as you move from the past toward the present and make note of the fact.

Whether your work is presented as a narrative, in a descriptive form, or as a literary criticism of the sources and the information they produce, it will some day be scrutinized, if only by the members of one's family.

Fifty Years

One point that surfaces early in this text is the brevity of American history in comparison to the European history that formed its backstory. Because of this brevity, American history is extremely dynamic. Two hundred thirty-two years of fits and starts brought America along a track that Europe had taken a thousand years to travel. This dynamic quality has also had a heavy impact on local history in the United States.

The last fifty years of American history brought two wars, one which highlighted a kind of national angst and the other seemingly forgotten: Vietnam and Korea. Few communities are untouched by one or both. Both appear to have been a part of a larger Cold War, where superpowers engaged in nuclear brinksmanship, as mankind found that its newly discovered capability to effectively destroy the planet gave diplomatic advantage.

The United States also noticed that its two largest silent populations, woman and the descendents of those Americans who suffered chattel slavery, were being denied the rights guaranteed under the Constitution. The late 1950s gave Americans photographic visions of small African American children being escorted into formerly all white schools by U.S. Marshals and November 2008 saw the election of an African American President by the largest margin of popular votes ever cast for a non-incumbent candidate.

The last fifty years were witness the failings of American government in the Watergate Scandal and the subsequent resignation of a President, to another attack on the United States and the beginning of yet another war—although war on a global scale, this war is of a different kind, undefined by national borders – providing, on one hand, a seeming confirmation that history is indeed cyclical and on the other hand, raising new questions about the nature of war and the relationship of cultures, and old questions about government infringing on the rights of its citizens. The post-Watergate culture of distrust for government naturally asked "what the government knew" before the attack, accompanied by accusations of war waged for the sake of political expediency, rather than for the "right reasons."

The very public failure of the system of political rewards and obligations – a part of politics since its inception in feudal times – was highlighted in the in the aftermath of Hurricane Katrina which transformed the states on the Gulf Coast into "America's Third World Country.

If a newspapers are history written under a deadline, then the changes in the methods of delivery of news over the last fifty years will also change the ways in which history is written, blurring the lines between local history and national history and expanding the sheer volume of sources available to the local historian as publications like the 150-year-old Rocky Mountain News surrender to the electronic media.

This doesn't argue for the abandonment of the historical method; rather, it calls for a closer scrutiny of these "new" sources using the same principles of critical thinking discussed earlier in this text. Immediacy and availability of sources, changes in the concept of community and the impact of recent larger historical events on local history and local historical processes should not distract the local historian from the need to discover how those local historical processes were affected by the results of those events, who was affected by those events, what the local results of those effects were, where these local events and effects occurred and when the effects were felt in the local community, however that community had been changed over the last half-century; rather, it should encourage the local historian to be even more careful and certain about sources.

A Final Note

American history is inexorably linked to English history for the first 175 years of its existence. The trade actions, political intrigues and the wars in which the English

"The Life & Times Of..."

involved themselves, from a century before the first English colonists set foot ashore a Jamestown, Virginia, until America declared its independence from England, shaped the people and the budding country becoming part of the character of that country. Today we, as historians, look at and for those who made America, and the places they called their community. When we write about them, we leave our generation's calling card to the future.

This text, hopefully, has shown the meaning of historical awareness and, just as hopefully, imparted some understanding of historical context and historical process, showing a way to interrogate sources using the historical method to wring valid hypotheses from those sources, which may be put to use by writing a history.

You may come to agree with historian William Hesseltine who said that writing history, "...is like trying to nail jelly to the wall." With luck, this book will help steady your hammer.

Citations

[1] Winston Churchill used a V sign in both versions to symbolize "V for Victory" during World War II Early on in the war he used palm in (sometimes with a cigar between the fingers). Later in the war he used palm out. It is thought that the aristocratic Churchill made the change after it was explained to him what it signified to the other classes in Britain. He developed the idea from a BBC campaign launched on 20 July 1941 with a message from Churchill for occupied Europe. Douglas Ritchie, of the BBC European Service, suggested adding an audible V using the Morse code rhythm—three dots and a dash – to the call-sign used by the BBC in its foreign language programs to occupied Europe for the rest of the war. The notes used for this audible V were those used as the opening bars of Beethoven's Fifth Symphony (V being the Roman numeral for 5).

The irony that the symphony was composed by a German was not lost on many of the audience.

[2] Hayden White in his text, *Metahistory: The Historical Imagination in Nineteenth Century Europe* (Johns Hopkins University Press), espoused the concept that writing history should be treated as if one were writing literary

criticism since, after all, sources and the narrative which grew from them, were little more than literary stories disguised as objective fact. Hayden White, *Metahistory: The Historical Imagination in Nineteenth-Century Europe,*

[3] Lynn Speer Lemisko, "The Historical Imagination: Collingwood in the Classroom" *Canadian Social Studies, Canada's National Social Studies Journal* Volume 38, Issue 2 (Winter 2004). [1] This excellent description was found on the website of Canadian Social Studies, (www.quasar.ualberta.ca/css) Canada's National Social Studies Journal – and was used by their permission.

Further Reading

Robert P. Swierenga, *Dutch Chicago: A History of Hollanders in the Windy City*, Wm. B. Eerdmans Publishing Co.

Roger Daniels, *Coming to America: A History of Immigration and Ethnicity in American Life*, HarperCollins, 2002

Evarts Boutell Greene, *The Foundations of American Nationality*, Kessinger Publishing, (2005)

Zadock Thompson, *History of Vermont: Natural, Civil and Statistical, in Three Parts, with an Appendix,* Published by The author, 1853 (available on Google Books)

William Durkee Williamson, *The History of the State of Maine: From Its First Discovery, A.D. 1602, to the Separation, A.D. 1820, Inclusive,* Glazier, Masters & Co., 1832

Richard Hofstadter, *Great Issues in American History: From the Revolution to the Civil War, 1765-1865,* Vintage, 1958

Wylene P. Dial, "The Dialect of The Appalachian People," *West Virginia History,* Volume 30, No. 2 (January 1969),

David Eltis, *Economic Growth and the Ending of the Transatlantic Slave Trade,* Oxford University Press (US), 1987

John D. Post, *The Last Great Subsistence Crisis in the Western World,* Books on Demand, 1977

William Bradford, *Bradford's History "Of Plimoth Plantation" From the Original Manuscript: with a Report of the Proceedings Incident to the Return of the*

Manuscript to Massachusetts By Massachusetts Office of the Secretary of State, Massachusetts General Court, Wright & Potter printing co., state printers, 1901

V. A. C. Gatrell, *The Hanging Tree: Execution and the English People 1770-1868*, Oxford University Press, 1996

Ralph Ellison, *The Invisible Man*, Modern Library, 1994, ISBN 0679601392

Geneviève Fabre, Robert G. O'Meally, *History and Memory in African-American Culture*, Oxford University Press, 1994

Robin Leigh Einhorn, *American Taxation, American Slavery,* University of Chicago Press, 2006 ISBN 0226194876, 9780226194875

Donna L. Franklin, William Julius Wilson, *Ensuring Inequality: The Structural Transformation of the African-American Family,* Oxford University Press US, 1997

Karen V. Hansen, Anita Ilta Garey, *Families in the U.S.: Kinship and Domestic Politics*, Temple University Press, 1998, ISBN 1566395909, 9781566395908

George Norman Clark, *English History: A Survey*, Clarendon Press, 1971, ISBN: 0198223390

Gilbert Joseph Garraghan, S.J., Jean Delanglez, Livia Appel, *A Guide to Historical Method*, Fordham University Press, 1948.

Louis Reichenthal Gottschalk, *Understanding History: A Primer of Historical Method*, Knopf, 1950

Donald A. Ritchie, *Doing Oral History: A Practical Guide*, Oxford University Press US, 2003

Hayden White, *Metahistory: The Historical Imagination in Nineteenth-Century Europe*, Johns Hopkins University Press, 1973

Pat Hudson, *History by Numbers: An Introduction to Quantitative Approaches*, Oxford University Press, 2000

"The Life & Times Of..."

Appendix 1: Online Resources in the United States

The appendices that follow include the web addresses of state archives and local historical societies, as well as a list of organizations that will prove worthwhile to the local and family historian. The information is current as of this writing.

National & State Archives & Historical Societies

The National Archives and Records Administration

http://www.archives.gov/

The Library of Congress

http://www.loc.gov/index.html

Most Highly Recommended:

"The Life & Times Of..."

The American Antiquarian Society's Local, County and State Histories Collection

http://www.americanantiquarian.org/localhist.htm

Alabama
Department of Archives & History
http://www.archives.alabama.gov
624 Washington Avenue, Montgomery, AL 36130
Mailing Address: P.O. Box 300100, Montgomery, AL 36130
Phone: Reference: (334) 242-4435
Phone: Records Center: (334) 242-4306
Fax: (334) 240-3433
TDD: (334) 242-3433 E-mail: *reference@archives.alabama.gov*

Alaska
State Archives
Http://www.archives.state.ak.us
Mailing Address: P.O. Box 110525, 141 Willoughby Avenue, Juneau, AK 99801
Phone: (907) 465-2270
Fax: (907) 465-2465
E-mail: archives@eed.state.ak.us

Alaska Historical Society
http://www.alaskahistoricalsociety.org/

Appendices

Arizona
State Library, Archives and Public Records
Arizona History and Archives Division
http://www.lib.az.us
Mailing Address: State Capitol, Suite 342, 1700 West Washington, Phoenix, AZ 85007
Phone: (602) 542-4159
Fax: (602) 542-4402
E-mail: See contact form at http://www.lib.az.us/archives/email.asp

Arizona Historical Society
http://www.arizonahistoricalsociety.org/

Arkansas
History Commission
http://www.ark-ives.com
Mailing Address: One Capitol Mall, Little Rock, AR 77201
Phone: (501) 682-6900

Arkansas Historical Association
http://www.uark.edu/depts/arkhist/home/

California
State Archives
http://www.ss.ca.gov/archives/archives.htm
Mailing Address: 1020 "O" Street, Sacramento, CA 95814
Phone: Reference Desk: (916) 653-2246
Phone: General Information: (916) 653-7715
Fax: (916) 653-7363

E-mail: *ArchivesWeb@ss.ca.gov* or see the form at http://www.ss.ca.gov/cgi-bin/print_form.cgi

California Historical Society
http://www.californiahistoricalsociety.org/main.html

Colorado
State Archives
http://www.colorado.gov/dpa/doit/archives
Mailing Address: 1313 Sherman Street, Room 1B-20, Denver, CO 80203
Phone: (303) 866-2358
Fax: (303) 866-2257
E-mail: *archives@state.co.us* or see form athttp://www.archives.state.co.us/forms/request.htm

Colorado Historical Society
http://www.coloradohistory.org/

Connecticut
State Archives
http://www.cslib.org/archives.htm
Mailing Address: Connecticut State Library, 231 Capitol Avenue, Hartford, CT 06106
Phone: (860) 757-6595
Phone: History and Genealogy Unit: (860) 757-6580
Fax: (860) 757-6542

Connecticut Historical Society
http://www.chs.org/

Delaware
Public Archives
http://www.state.de.us/sos/dpa/
Mailing Address: 121 Duke of York Street, Dover, DE 19901
Phone: (302) 744-5000
Fax: (302) 739-6710
E-mail: archives@state.de.us

Historical Society of Delaware
http://www.hsd.org/

Florida
Bureau of Archives & Records Management, Division of Library & Information Services
http://dlis.dos.state.fl.us/barm/fsa.html
Mailing Address: 500 South Bronough Street, Tallahassee, FL 32399
Phone: (850) 245-6700
E-mail: *barm@dos.state.fl.us*

Florida Historical Society
http://www.florida-historical-soc.org/

Georgia
Archives

"The Life & Times Of..."

http://www.georgiaarchives.org
Mailing Address: 5800 Jonesboro Road, Morrow, GA 30260
Phone: (678) 364-3700
E-mail: See contact page athttp://www.georgiaarchives.org/menu/contact_us/default.htm

Georgia Historical Society
http://www.florida-historical-soc.org/

Georgia Association of Historians
http://a-s.clayton.edu/gah/

Hawaii
Historic Records Branch
http://www.state.hi.us/dags/archives/"
Mailing Address: Kekauluohi Building, Iolani Palace Grounds, Honolulu, HI 96813
Phone: Reference Desk: (808) 586-0329
Fax: (808) 586-0330
E-mail: *archives@hawaii.gov*

Hawaiian Historical Society
http://www.hawaiianhistory.org/

Idaho
State Historical Society Library & Archives
http://www.idahohistory.net/library_archives.html
Mailing Address: Public Archives and Research Library, 2205 Old Penitentiary Road, Boise, ID 83712

Appendices

Phone: History & Genealogy: (208) 334-3356
Phone: Oral History: (208) 334-3863
Phone: Archives: (208) 334-2620
Fax:: **(**208) 334-3198
Email: Reference: *sbarrett@ishs.state.id.us*

Idaho State Historical Society
http://www.idahohistory.net/

Illinois
State Archives
http://www.sos.state.il.us/departments/archives/archives.html
Mailing Address: Norton Building, Capitol Complex, Springfield, IL 62756
Phone: (217) 782-4682
Fax: (217) 524-3930
E-mail: See form
at *https://www.ilsos.gov/GenealogyMWeb/refform.html*

Illinois State Historical Society
http://www.historyillinois.org/

Indiana
State Archives
http://www.in.gov/icpr/archives
Mailing Address: 6440 East 30th Street, Indianapolis, Indiana 46219
Phone: (317) 591-5222
Fax: (317) 591-5324

"The Life & Times Of..."

E-mail: *arc@icpr.in.gov* or see form at *http://www.in.gov/icpr/contact/*

Indiana Historical Society
http://www.indianahistory.org/

Iowa
State Library of Iowa
http://www.statelibraryofiowa.org/index.html
Mailing Address: Ola Babcock Miller Building, 1112 E. Grand Ave., Des Moines, IA 50319-0233
Phone: (515) 281-4105 or 1 (800) 248-4483
Fax: (515) 281-6191
E-mail: See forms
at *http://www.statelibraryofiowa.org/services/askalibrarian*

State Historical Society of Iowa
http://www.iowahistory.org/

Kansas
State Historical Society
http://www.kshs.org/
Mailing Address: 6425 Southwest Sixth Avenue, Topeka, KS 66615
Phone: (785) 272-8681 ext. 117
Fax: (785) 272-8682
TTY: (785) 272-8683
E-mail: *information@kshs.org* or see form
at *http://www.kshs.org/contact/emailref.php*

Kansas State Historical Society

Appendices

http://www.kshs.org/

Kentucky
Department for Libraries & Archives
http://www.kdla.ky.gov
Mailing Address: P.O. Box 537, Frankfort, KY 40602
Phone: **(502) 564-8300**
Fax: **(502) 564-5773**

Kentucky Historical Society
http://history.ky.gov/

Louisiana
State Archives
http://www.sec.state.la.us/archives/archives/archives-index.htm
Mailing Address: 3851 Essen Lane, Baton Rouge, LA 70809
Phone: (225) 922-1000
E-mail: *archives@sos.louisiana.gov*

Louisiana Historical Society
http://www.louisianahistoricalsociety.org/

Maine
State Archives
http://www.state.me.us/sos/arc/
Mailing Address: 84 State House Station, Augusta, ME 04333-0084
Phone: (207) 287-5788

193

"The Life & Times Of..."

Fax: (207) 287-5739
E-mail: *anthony.douin@maine.gov*

Maine Historical Society
http://www.mainehistory.org/

Maryland
State Archives
http://www.mdarchives.state.md.us/
Mailing Address: 350 Rowe Boulevard, Annapolis, MD 21401
Phone: (410) 260-6400
Tollfree MD only: 1-800-235-4045
Fax: (410) 974-2525
E-mail: *archives@mdsa.net*

Maryland Historical Society
http://www.mdhs.org/

Massachusetts
Archives
http://www.sec.state.ma.us/arc/arcidx.htm
Mailing Address: Secretary of Commonwealth, Massachusetts Archives, 220 Morrissey Boulevard, Boston, MA 02125
Phone: (617) 727-2816
Fax: (617)288-8429
E-mail: *archives@sec.state.ma.us*

Massachusetts Historical Society
http://masshist.org/

Michigan
Department of History, Arts and Libraries
Michigan Historical Society
http://www.michigan.gov/archivesofmi
Mailing Address: Archives of Michigan, 702 Kalamazoo Street, P.O. Box 30740
Phone: (517) 373-1408
Fax: (517) 241-1658
TDD: (517) 373-1592
E-mail: *archives@michigan.gov*

Historical Society of Michigan
http://www.hsofmich.org/

Minnesota
State Archives
http://www.mnhs.org/preserve/records/index.html
Mailing Address: Minnesota Historical Society, 345 Kellogg Boulevard West, St. Paul, MN 55102
Phone: (651) 297-4502
Fax: (651) 296-9961
E-mail: *archives@mnhs.org*

Mississippi
Department of Archives & History
http://www.mdah.state.ms.us/
Mailing Address:P.O. Box 571, Jackson, MS 39205-0571
Phone: Archives and Library: (601) 576-6964
Phone: General Information: (601) 576-6850
Phone: Historic Preservation Division: (601) 576-6955

Fax: (601) 576-6975
E-mail: *refdesk@mdah.state.ms.us*. Please read the guidelines before sending email.

Mississippi Historical Society
http://mshistory.k12.ms.us/

Missouri
State Archives
http://www.sos.mo.gov/archives/
Mailing Address: 600 W. Main, P.O. Box 1747, Jefferson City, MO 65102
Phone: (573) 751-3280
Fax: (573) 526-7333
E-mail: *archref@sos.mo.gov* or see form at *http://www.sos.mo.gov/archives/resources/email.asp*

Missouri Historical Society
http://www.mohistory.org/
Montana
Historical Society
http://www.his.state.mt.us
Mailing Address: P.O. Box 201201, 225 North Roberts Street, Helena, MT 59620
Phone: (406) 444-2694
Fax: Main: (406) 444-2696
Fax: Library: (406) 444-5297
E-mail: mhslibrary@mt.gov

Nebraska
Library/Archives Division

http://www.nebraskahistory.org/lib-arch/index.htm
Mailing Address:Nebraska State Historical Society, P.O. Box 82554, 1500 R Street, Lincoln, NE 68501
Phone: (402) 471-4751
Fax: (402) 471-3100
E-mail: *lanshs@nebraskahistory.org*

Nebraska State Historical Society
http://www.nebraskahistory.org/

Nevada
State Library & Archives
http://nevadaculture.org/docs/nsla/archives/"
Mailing Address: 100 North Stewart Street, Carson City, NV 89701
Phone: (775) 684-3310
Fax: (775) 684-3311
E-mail: *sesearcy@clan.lib.nv.us* or see for at
http://nevadaculture.org/docs/email/archivesform.htm

Nevada Historical Society
http://nevadaculture.org/docs/museums/reno/his-soc.htm

New Hampshire
Archives & Records Management
http://www.sos.nh.gov/archives/
Mailing Address: 71 South Fruit Street, Concord, NH 03301
Phone: (603) 271-2236
Fax: (603) 271-2272

New Hampshire Historical Society
http://www.nhhistory.org/

New Mexico
State Records Center & Archives
http://www.nmcpr.state.nm.us
Mailing Address: 1205 Camino Carlos Rey, Santa Fe, NM 87505
Phone: Historical Services Division: (505) 476-7908
Phone: State Records Center: (505) 476-7903
Fax: Historical Services Division: (505) 476-7909
Fax: State Records Center: (505) 476-7910
E-mail: *archives@state.nm.us*

Historical Society of New Mexico
http://www.hsnm.org/default.asp?DomName=hsnm.org

New Jersey
Public Records and Archives
http://www.state.nj.us/state/darm/
Mailing Address: State Archives: 225 West State Street-Level 2, P.O. Box 307, Trenton, NJ 08625-0307
Phone: State Records Center: (609) 530-3200
Fax: State Archives:(609) 396-2454
Fax: State Records Center: (609) 530-6121 E-mail: State Archives: *archives.reference@sos.state.nj.us*
E-mail: State Records Center: *records.management@sos.state.nj.us*

New Jersey Historical Society http://www.jerseyhistory.org/

Appendices

New York
State Archives
http://www.archives.nysed.gov/aindex.shtml
Mailing Address: New York State Education Department, Cultural Education Center, Albany, NY 12230
Phone: Archives Reference Information: (518) 474-8955
E-mail: Archives Reference Information: *archref@mail.nysed.gov*

New York Historical Society
https://www.nyhistory.org/web/

North Carolina
State Archives
http://www.ah.dcr.state.nc.us/archives
Mailing Address: 4614 Mail Service Center, Raleigh, NC 27699-4614
Phone: (919) 807-7310
Fax: (919) 733-1354
E-mail: *archives@ncmail.net*

North Dakota
State Archives & Historical Research Library
http://www.state.nd.us/hist/sal.htm
Mailing Address: 612 East Boulevard Avenue, Bismarck, ND 58505-0830
Phone: (701) 328-2091
Fax: (701) 328-2650
E-mail: *archives@state.nd.us*

State Historical Society of North Dakota

"The Life & Times Of..."

http://www.nd.gov/hist/index.html

Ohio
Historical Society, Archives/Library
http://www.ohiohistory.org/resource/statearc/index.html
Mailing Address: Research Services Department, 1982 Velma Avenue, Columbus, OH 43211
Phone: (614) 297-2510
E-mail: *reference@ohiohistory.org* or see contact form at http://www.ohiohistory.org/contact.html

Oklahoma
State Archives
http://www.odl.state.ok.us/oar
Mailing Address: 200 Northeast Eighteenth Street, Oklahoma City, OK 73105-3298
Phone: (405) 522-3579
Fax:(405) 522-3583
Email: See staff listing
at *http://www.odl.state.ok.us/oar/contacts/index.html*

Oklahoma Historical Society
http://www.okhistory.org/

Oregon
State Archives
http://arcweb.sos.state.or.us/
Mailing Address: 800 Summer Street NE, Salem, OR 97310
Phone: (503) 373-0701

Fax: **(503) 373-0953**
E-mail: *reference.archives@state.or.us*

Oregon Historical Society
http://www.ohs.org/

Pennsylvania
State Archives
http://www.phmc.state.pa.us/bah/dam/overview.htm
Mailing Address: 350 North Street, Harrisburg, PA 17120-0090. Also, see mail reference form at *http://www.phmc.state.pa.us/bah/dam/mailreflet.html*
Phone: (717) 783-3281

Historical Society of Pennsylvania
http://www.hsp.org/

Rhode Island
State Archives
http://www.state.ri.us/archives/
Mailing Address: 337 Westminster Street, Providence, RI 02903
Phone: (401) 222-2353
Fax: (401) 222-3199
E-mail: *reference@sec.state.ri.us*

Rhode Island Historical Society
http://www.rihs.org/

South Carolina
State Archives & History Center

http://www.state.sc.us/scdah/homepage.htm
Mailing Address: 8301 Parklane Road, Columbia, SC 29223
Phone: General Information: (803) 896-6100
Phone: Reference Services: (803) 896-6104 or (803) 896-6105
Fax: (803) 896-6198
E-mail: See contact form
at *http://www.state.sc.us/scdah/refquery.htm*

South Carolina Historical Society
http://www.southcarolinahistoricalsociety.org/

South Dakota
State Archives
http://www.sdhistory.org/arc/archives.htm
Mailing Address: 900 Governors Drive, Pierre, SD 57501-2217
Phone: (605) 773-3804
Fax: (605) 773-6041
E-mail: *archref@state.sd.us*

South Dakota State Historical Society
http://www.sdhistory.org/

Tennessee
State Library & Archives
http://www.tennessee.gov/tsla/
Mailing Address: 403 Seventh Avenue North, Nashville, TN 37243-0312
Phone: (615) 741-2764

Appendices

Fax: (615) 532-2472
E-mail: *reference.tsla@state.tn.us*

Tennessee Historical Society
http://www.tennesseehistory.org/

Texas
State Library & Archives Commission
http://www.tsl.state.tx.us/
Mailing Address: P.O. Box 12927, Austin, TX 78711
Phone: State Archives: (512) 463-5480
Phone: Reference: (512) 463-5455
E-mail: State Archives: *archinfo@tsl.state.tx.us*
Email: Reference: *reference.desk@tsl.state.tx.us*

Texas State Historical Association
http://www.tshaonline.org/

Utah
State Archives
http://archives.utah.gov/
Mailing Address: Utah State Archives and Records Service, 346 S Rio Grande, Salt Lake City, UT 84101-1106
Phone: (801) 531-3848
Fax: (801) 531-3854
E-mail: See contact form
at *http://historyresearch.utah.gov/question.htm*

Utah State Historical Society
http://history.utah.gov/

Vermont
State Archives
http://vermont-archives.org/
Mailing Address: Office of the Secretary of State, 26 Terrace Street, Montpelier, VT 05609-1101
Phone: (802) 828-2308
Fax: (802) 828-1135
E-mail: *archives@sec.state.vt.us*

Vermont Historical Society
http://www.vermonthistory.org/

Virginia
Archives Research Services
http://www.lva.lib.va.us
Mailing Address: Library of Virginia, 800 East Broad Street, Richmond, VA 23219
Phone: Archives: (804) 692-3888
Fax: Archives: (804) 692-3556
E-mail: See contact form
at *http://www.lva.lib.va.us/whatwedo/archemailform.asp*

Virginia Historical Society
http://www.vahistorical.org/

Washington
State Archives
http://secstate.wa.gov/archives
Mailing Address: P.O. Box 40238, Olympia, WA 98504
Phone: Research: (360) 586-1492

Appendices

E-mail: State Archivist: *archives@secstate.wa.gov* or Research Requests and Information on Public Records: *research@secstate.wa.gov*

Washington State Historical Society
http://www.wshs.org/

West Virginia
State Archives
http://www.wvculture.org/history/wvsamenu.html
Mailing Address: Archives & History Library, The Cultural Center, 1900 Kanawha Boulevard East, Charleston, WV 25305-0300
Phone: (304) 558-0230

Wisconsin
State Historical Society
http://wisconsinhistory.org/libraryarchives/
Mailing Address: Archives Reference, 816 State Street, Madison, WI 53706
Phone: (608) 264-6460
Fax: (608) 264-6472
E-mail: See contact form at *http://wisconsinhistory.org/libraryarchives/reference_form.asp?program=ar*

Wisconsin Historical Society
http://www.wisconsinhistory.org/

"The Life & Times Of..."

Wyoming
State Archives
http://wyoarchives.state.wy.us/index.htm
Mailing Address: Barrett Building, 2301 Central Avenue, Cheyenne, WY 82002
Phone: (307) 777-7826
Fax: (307) 777-7044
E-mail: *wyarchive@state.wy.us*
Wyoming State Historical Society
http://www.wyshs.org/

Appendix 2:
Online Resources Outside the United States

Sources In Great Britain and Ireland

The National Archives (UK) has records going back as far as 1259. They include every surviving document of the government many documents (wills, deeds and charters are some examples) of private citizens in England. Many are available online or may be downloaded for a small fee. The National Archives of the United Kingdom also houses records for Wales and in part, Ireland. The website is located at: **http://www.nationalarchives.gov.uk**

The British Library has records, books and artifacts that pre-date the Norman Conquest of 1066, as well as much information for the person in pursuit of an understanding of the historical context of a British connection.

The National Archives of Scotland houses records from the 12th to the 21st Century, which touch on every aspect of life in Scotland. Their website is at: **http://www.**

nas.gov.uk

The National Archives of Ireland maintain that document its historical evolution and the creation of its national identity. The also archives include extensive and substantial information and documentation on Irish genealogy as well as Transportation Records. Their address is **http://www.nationalarchives.ie**

Canada and Mexico

Library and Archives Canada combines the national library and the national archives of Canada in one website, in both English and French:
http://www.collectionscanada.gc.ca/

The National Archives of Mexico, (El Archivo General de la Nación) are in Spanish and house a wealth of information and quite a bit of specialized family history. The archives are located online at: **www.Agn.gov.mx**

Central America

Not all national archives are available online; past political instabilities have resulted in the destruction of documents, restrictions on documents or off-site housing of documents at libraries and archives in the United States.

Guatemalan National Police Archives: The National Police were disbanded after country's 1996 Peace Accords and were replaced by the National Civil Police. These records can be found online at the George Washington University

National Security Archive.
http://www.gwu.edu/~nsarchiv/NSAEBB/NSAEBB170/index.htm

Portal, National Archives, Guatemala:
http://www.lanic.utexas.edu/project/tavera/guatemala/

The National Archives of Honduras, covering a date range from 1605 to 1938, are on microfilm, available at the University of Texas Library in Arlington. Guides to selected materials are available at the UT-A website at: **http://library.uta.edu/findingAids/HondurasMF.jsp**

El Salvador's *Archivo General de la Nacion* is available at: **(http://www.agn.gob.sv/)**

"The Life & Times Of..."

Index

Numerical References

442nd Regimental Combat Team, 84

1917 Flu Epidemic, 147

A

accumulation of hypotheses, 158

Adaptive reuse, 73

Aerial photography, 153

African, 49, 63

Africans, 33, 34

Agincourt, 28

Alfred the Great, 27, 49

alignment of roads, 70

Alleghenies, 63

American Revolution, 22, 24, 50

anachronism, 51

Ancestry.com, 116

Anglican Church, 69

Anne, 30

Ansel Adams, 83

archaeological remains, 113

archiving an oral history, 110

archivist, 116

argument from analogy, 117, 121

argument to the best explanation, 117, 121

arithmetic mean, 148

B

back yards, 16

based on a true story, 17, 162

Battle of Trafalgar, 96

bedroom communities, 69

benefices, 27

better explanation, 119

Black Death, 27

Blue Ridge Mountains, 63

Boston, 63

British Library, 205

C

Case, 139, 140

categorical data, 131

Catholic Church, 69

causal analysis, 134

Charles II, 30

Charleston, South Carolina, 25, 69

Chaucer, 49

Church of Jesus Christ of Latter Day Saints, 116

circumstantial evidence, 158

Civil Rights Act of 1964, 85

Cladistics, 102

Common Sense, 20

Communities Resulting from Prejudice, 82

community, 70, 78, 80

Community, 61, 77, 79

computer, 122, 130, 153

Constitution, 84

County, 69county records office, 68

court of public opinion, 83

Cowan Shulman, 110

D

Data matrix, 140

Data set, 139, 147

December 7, 1941, 83

Decline and Fall of the Roman Empire, 92

Délégation Générale à la Langue Française, 50

deliberate distortion, 117

demography, 152

Descriptive statistics, 133

Determining Which, 113

disinformation, 117

dispersions, 151

Distribution, 144, 145, 146, 147

Doing Oral History. See Cowan Shulman

Don't Panic, 114

Douglas Adams

    Author, Hitchhiker's Guide to the Galaxy, 114

E

E. B. Greene, 20

E. P. Thompson, 76

Edward Gibbon., 93

El Cazador, 22

element of negation, 119

Ellison, Ralph, 82, 87, 179

Emancipation Proclamation, 84

employment, 75, 78

enforceable local law, 69

England, 63, 75, 205

English Civil Wars, 108

213

essential synthesis of People and Place, 79

ethnicity, 78

Executive Order 9066, 83

existence by implication, 120

external criticism, 99

Eyewitness Evidence, 102

F

Fair Labor Standards Act of 1939, 135

family history, 62, 100, 167

famine, 34, 35, 36, 38, 44, 153

famines, 27, 35, 36

Field, 141

Finnish Great Famine of 1696, 35

first 'great famine' in Europe, 35

forgery, 117

France, 63

"free slave" communities, 82

French Protestants, 24

French Quarter, 48

frequency distribution, 144, 146, 147, 148, 150

Frequency distribution, 144, 147

G

gentry, 77

Geographic Information Systems, 153

geographical limits, 62

Gilbert J. Garraghan, 98

GIS, 153, 154. *See* Geographic Information Systems

Glorious Revolution, 30

Glorious Revolution', 30

Google Earth, 153

graph, 132, 133, 136, 137, 141

Gray, 49

Great Depression, 165, 166

Great Famine of 1315-1317., 35

Great Famine of Estonia, 35

Great Smoky, 63

greater explanatory scope, 118

guilds or unions, 78

Gullah, 82

H

half-truth, 117

hanging, 52

higher criticism, 99, 101

historic employment patterns, 153

historical context, 75, 162, 164, 165

Historical Context, 51

historical empiricism. *See* Historical Imagination

historical imagination, 159, 161, 162, 166, 172

historical process, 53

Holocaust, 109

Huguenot, 25

Huguenots, 24, 25

hypothesis, 118, 119, 120, 158, 159

I

immigrants, 47

income, 131, 135, 153

indentured servants, 33

Indentured servitude, 33

industrialization, 65, 153

Inferential statistics, 133

internal criticism, 99

interpretation, 111, 123, 124

Interpreting Sources, 163

Interrogating &, 123

interval data, 132, 133

Ireland, 205

Irish genealogy, 205

J

Japan, 83

Japanese-American internment, 109

Japanese-Americans, 83

JDLR, 105

Jefferson, 23, 54

John D. Post, 39, 58, 178

K

King Charles, 108

King James II, 30

L

L. P. Hartley, 51

landscape, 74, 77, 80

language, 48, 49, 50, 78

large scale studies, 139

legal boundaries, 67

Linacre College, 152

Little Ice Age, 35, 36, 38

Index

local governance, 78

London & Company, 32

London & Virginia, 31

London & Virginia Company, 31, 75

London Company, 32

Louis Gottschalk, 99, 106

Louisiana, 69, 100

Louisiana Purchase, 24, 25, 48, 54, 57

lower criticism, 99, 102

Lynn Speer Lemisko, 161

M

Maine, 20

Manzanar War Relocation Center, 83

Market towns, 27

Mary, Queen of Scots, 30

Mayflower, 32, 76

Mayflower Compact, 32

mean, 77, 117, 124, 148, 149, 151, 160, 171

median, 148, 149

Medieval Latin, 18

metes and bounds, 68

Metropolitan Atlanta Rapid Transit Authority, 69

Mississippi River, 100

Missouri Compromise, 21

modal distribution. See mode

mode, 97, 148, 150

Mount Tambura, 39

multiple layers of information. See GIS Systems

217

N

Napoleonic Wars, 44

National Archives (UK), 205

National Archives of Ireland, 205

National Archives of Scotland, 205

National Archives of the United Kingdom, 100, 205

National Boundaries, 70

national origin, 78

Native Americans, 50

Natural features, 74

Neighborhood. See Political Subdivisions

Netherlands, 31, 35

network of relationships, 79

New France, 25

New Orleans, 22, 23, 48, 49, 69

New Paltz, New York, 25

New Spain, 22

New York, 21, 24, 39, 63

Nominal data, 131, 133

Norman Conquest, 27, 205

Northeast Territory, 63

Northwest Territory, 22

nuclear families, 77

numeric data, 131

Numeric data, 132

O

observational statement, 119

Ohio Valley, 63

only surviving documentation, 143

onomastics, 152

oral history, 19, 99

Oral history, 110

Oral History, 109, 110, 126

Oral tradition, 111, 112

Ordinal data, 131

outside help, 167

overlap between categories or class intervals, 148

P

paleography, 18

pandemics, 41, 133, 153

Pat Hudson, 152, 181

patronage, 26

Peace of Paris, 22

Pearl Harbor, 83

Peasants' Revolt of 1381, 28

peonage, 34

people, xv, 25, 33, 34, 35, 48, 50, 52, 61, 74, 75, 78, 79, 80

Philadelphia, 63

pie chart, 133

Pilgrims, 30, 32

Piltdown Man, 102

Place, 67

plausibility, 119

Plymouth Colony, 30, 31

political subdivisions, 68, 69

population shifts, 153

prejudices, 48, 78

Prerogative Court of Canterbury, 108

present, observable data, 118

President Franklin D. Roosevelt, 83

primary sources, 92, 107, 115

Prince William of Orange, 30

probability, 99, 100, 121

propaganda, 95, 117, 124

Prosopography, 151

Prosopography of Anglo Saxon England, 152

Provenance, 98

Q

qualitative data, 131

Quantitative analysis, 130, 131

quantitative data, 131

Queen Elizabeth I, 28, 49

R

racial and ethnic minorities, 109

railroads, 73

ratio data, 132

Regional Transportation District, 69

religion, xv, 48, 78

religious freedom, 30, 32

relocation camps, 84

Richard II, 28

RKO, 163

road, 70

Robert Swierenga, 130

Robin George Collingwood, 160

Index

ruling class, 63

S

Samuel Hays, 130

Satchel Paige, 148

scaffold crowd, 52

secondary sources, 93

Secondary sources, 92

See E. P. Thompson.

Selection of resources, 117

Selective *use* of resources, 116

Separatists, 30, 31

serving class, 63

Shakespeare, 49

silent class, 63

skepticism, 124, 164

slavery, 63

Slavery, 33, 34

social demarcations, 77

Sources & Critical Thinking, 95

Southern Mountain Dialect, 49

Soviet Gulags, 109

speculation and supposition, 119, 120

Standard deviation, 151

statistical inference, 117, 121

Stemmatics, 102

sub-communities, 77

subjective element, 160

success of circumstantial evidence, 158

Sutter's Creek, 64

Synthesis, 157

T

tabular, 137, 145

The Computer in, 129

the Crown, 108

the decision of the historian, 158

The Go-Between, 51

The Hanging Tree, 52, 59, 179

The Invisible Man. See Ellison, Ralph

The Oral History Association, 111

the peculiar institution, 63

The Prince, 53

The Year Without a Summer, 39

Theories of Meaning, 162

thick communities, 78

thin communities, 78

Thomas Paine, 20

Time-series, 134

Treaty of Paris, 22

U

United Kingdom, 62

United States, xvi, xv, 18, 62

University of Oxford, 152

unwitting witnesses, 108

upward mobility, 76

Urban Planning, 70

V

V.A.C. Gatrell, 52

V.S.L.M, 122

validated hypothesis, 122

Variable, 140

Index

variance, 72, 151

Vector, 141

Viking, 27

Vlad the Impaler, 53

Votum Solvit Libens Merito, 122

W

walk the ground, 154

War, 43

Washington, 39

William Shakespeare, 94

Winfield, Kansas, 74

World War II, 84

worldview, 75, 78

Writing history, 157

About the Author

Trained in historic preservation and local history in Charleston, South Carolina, Will Carpenter is a practicing local historian.

He lives in the hills of Tennessee with three formerly feral cats.

"The Life & Times Of..."

Other Books by Will Carpenter

- *Sea Stories and Other Lies*

- *The Prosopography of Native America*

    A four volume set about Native American familial and tribal relationships, *available in March 2012*

Visit our website at http://www.historyworksbooks.com

"The Life & Times Of..."

www.ingramcontent.com/pod-product-compliance
Lightning Source LLC
Chambersburg PA
CBHW020229170426
43201CB00007B/370